# HOW TO WIN AT
# OMAHA HIGH-LOW POKER

# About the Author

Mike wrote the best selling textbook on Omaha poker, *Cappelletti on Omaha*. His column for *Card Player* magazine has appeared every two weeks from 1989 to the present. In 1995, the first collection of Mike's best poker articles was published as *The Best of Cappelletti on Omaha*. He is often referred to as the leading authority on Omaha.

Mike Cappelletti was formerly a lawyer for the U.S. Department of Justice. He is also a well known bridge player who has represented the United States in international competition.

In the 1980s, *The New York Times* referred to Mike and his wife as the best husband-and-wife bridge partnership in the world. *People Magazine* then featured the Cappelletti's in their four-page "Couples Section."

# HOW TO WIN AT
# OMAHA HIGH-LOW POKER

## Mike Cappelletti

## CARDOZA PUBLISHING

**FIRST EDITION**

Library of Congress Catalog Card No: 2003109492
ISBN:1-58042-114-8

Visit our new web site (www.cardozapub.com) or write us
for a full list of Cardoza books, advanced and computer strategies.

**CARDOZA PUBLISHING**
P.O. Box 1500, Cooper Station, New York, NY 10276
Phone (800)577-WINS
email: cardozapub@aol.com
**www.cardozapub.com**

*With great appreciation, this book is dedicated to my publisher, Avery Cardoza, whose tireless assistance and many valuable suggestions made this book possible.*

# TABLE OF CONTENTS

# INTRODUCTION

I'm going to show you how to play and win big money at the hottest new poker game today: Omaha High-Low Poker! There is a simple reason why this game has become so popular among players and it is this—if you know what you're doing, you can win more money playing Omaha High-Low than any other poker game. That's why it is my game of choice.

But to be a winner, you have to learn the strategies and techniques that are unique to Omaha High-Low, which I am going to show you in this book. It's jam-packed with more than seventy hard-hitting sections, fine-tuned to show you how to consistently make money at Omaha.

Everything you need to know is here: From the rules of play and the best starting hands, to the strategies for the flop, turn, and river. I will show you how to maximize every single hand into the most profitable situation. This is a power course on every aspect of being a winning player. You'll learn how to read the board for high, low and dangerous draws, the different flop types you should be familiar with, single and double promo raises, duplication, defending the blind, driving hands, pushing and pulling hands, making big moves, and so much more—including professional secrets your fellow players will not know.

To make learning easy, I've included charts and many sample hands.

You can make a lot of money playing Omaha. So read on—the path to winning and profits is in your hands!

# UNDERSTANDING THE AVERAGE WIN

Throughout the book I will be comparing average win percentages for specific hands and situations with overall average wins based solely on the number of players (and not any particular hands) to illustrate whether the specific hand examined is profitable or not.

For example, if there is a four person hand, the specific hand against three opponents, I may point out in parenthesis that 25% is the average win (25% is average). This average win calculates only the expected win given the number of players in the pot—irregardless of any particular hand—to show whether the hand being examined wins more than the average win (is profitable), or wins less than the average win (is unprofitable).

Average wins are as follows:

| Players | Average Win |
|---------|-------------|
| 2 | 50% |
| 3 | 33% |
| 4 | 25% |
| 5 | 20% |
| 6 | 16.7% |
| 7 | 14.3% |
| 8 | 12.5% |
| 9 | 11.1% |
| 10 | 10% |

# 1 HOW TO PLAY OMAHA HIGH-LOW

Omaha high-low is a variation of four-card Omaha poker in which the pot is split equally between the best poker hand (**high hand** or **high**) and the best low hand (**low hand** or **low**). The ranking of five-card poker hands is generally the same in all forms of poker. Here's a table listing highest to lowest in standard high poker, for those who don't know:

**Royal flush**
The five consecutive highest cards in the same suit
10♥ J♥ Q♥ K♥ A♥

**Straight flush**
Five consecutive cards in same suit
7♦ 8♦ 9♦ 10♦ J♦

**Four-of-a-kind**
Four cards of same denomination
7♦ 7♥ 7♣ 7♠ 2♥

**Full house**
Three-of-a-kind and one pair
K♦ K♥ K♠ 8♣ 8♥ (kings full)

**Flush**
ALL five cards of same suit
2♥ 4♥ 7♥ 8♥ Q♥

**Straight**
Five consecutive cards
4♥ 5♠ 6♥ 7♣ 8♥ (8-high straight)

**Three-of-a-kind**
Three cards of same denomination
5♥ 5♣ 5♦ 3♥ 2♦ (trip 5s)

**Two pair**
Two pairs
9♣ 9♥ 2♦ 2♣ 3♥ (9s-up)

**One pair**
Two cards of same denomination
Q♥ Q♣ 3♦ 5♣ 6♦ (pair of queens)

**High-card**
no pairs or other of the above
K♦ J♣ 8♥ 6♠ 3♦ (king-jack high)

As you can see from this table, a five-card poker hand containing three 5s (three-of-a-kind) is better than a hand containing two aces and two queens, (two-pair). But if both competing hands are two-pairs, then the hand with the highest pair wins. For example, two kings and two 3s (kings over) is better than two queens and two jacks (queens over).

If you already know the rules of Omaha and understand that there are blinds instead of antes, you may safely skip over the next two sections on rules and structure.

# A BRIEF SUMMARY OF OMAHA RULES
Omaha poker is generally played as follows:

Each player is dealt four down cards, concealed from the view of the other players. These four cards constitute a player's entire private Omaha hand. Each player's entire poker hand consists of nine cards—the four down cards plus five common board cards, dealt face up in the center of the table. All players use the same five common board cards.

If two or more players remain in the pot for the showdown after the last round of betting, the fourth, the best five-card poker hand wins. Five-card poker hands are made only by using *exactly two* cards from your hand, from your four private cards, and *exactly three* of the five board cards.

At straight high Omaha, the five cards which make the best poker hand, using two hand cards and three of the five common board cards, win the whole pot. At Omaha high-low, the five cards which make the best poker hand win at least half of the pot. The five cards which make the lowest low hand win the other half of the pot. The player may use whatever two cards of the four in his hand to form the high hand or the low including the same two for both the high and the low hands. If no hand qualifies for low (see qualifying conditions below), then the best high hand wins the whole pot.

Let's describe a hand of Omaha in detail.

**1.** In casinos, a dealer button is used to designate the dealer's position. The button, as this position is called, rotates clockwise around the table after each hand. The cards are dealt clockwise starting with the player to the left of the dealer, or button. Each round of betting proceeds clockwise, in the same manner, starting to the left of the dealer.

**2.** Each player is dealt four down cards, also called private cards or hidden cards.

**3.** Everyone looks at his own four down cards. There is a first round of betting before the flop, which we'll get to in a moment, starting to the left of the dealer. Each player has the option of folding, calling, or raising in turn, as in all forms of poker. Of course, at this point, no one knows which five cards will turn up on the board.

**4.** Assuming that more than one player remains after the first round of betting, the dealer deals three cards face-up on the table. These three board cards are collectively called the **flop**, and they belong equally to all players. Now that you've seen seven of your eventual nine cards, there is a second round of betting. You should consider how well the three-card flop combines with all two-card combinations in your private hand.

**5.** Assuming that more than one player remains after the second round of betting—after the flop—the dealer adds a fourth board card face-up on the table, called the **turn** card. There is a third round of betting.

**6.** The dealer adds a fifth and final board card face-up on the table, called the **river** card. Again, all of the five board cards belong equally to all players. At this point, each remaining player visualizes his best five card poker hand using any three of the five communal board cards and any two of his four private hand cards, which only he can use.

**7.** After the river card is dealt, there is another round of betting, the fourth and final round. If two or more players call this final round of betting, which is called the **showdown**, here's what happens:

• If you're playing Omaha high, whoever has the best five-card poker hand wins the pot. In the event of a tie, the pot is divided equally.

• If you're playing Omaha high-low, then the lowest low hand splits the pot equally with the best high poker hand. The lowest low hand also must be made using exactly two hand cards and three board cards.

Note that Omaha high-low is usually played such that an 8 or lower low hand, a hand in which the highest card is, at most, an 8, is required to qualify for the low half of the pot. If no hand in the showdown is an 8 or lower hand, then the best high poker hand wins the entire pot. Five cards of different denominations 8 or lower are required to make a low hand, and straights and flushes are ignored. Thus, the lowest possible low hand is 5 4 3 2 A—note that an ace is lower than a deuce. That hand is often called a **wheel**, since those same cards also constitute a straight which might win high as well.

A much less popular variation of Omaha high-low, sometimes called "California," requires that players treat aces as high cards only, that is, higher than kings and *not* lower than 2s—even for low-making purposes, and all five-card hand and board combinations which make straights or flushes as high hands only. Under those rules, the best low hand is 7 5 4 3 2. When only 2s through 8s are considered low cards, low hands "8 or better" occur much less frequently.

## GAME STRUCTURE

Omaha, hold 'em, and other board poker games with five communal board cards are usually played without antes. Instead, the first two (sometimes three) players to act are required to put up either a unit bet or a half unit bet. This forced bet is called a **blind,** an appropriate name, since this bet is posted before the players look at the cards in their private hands.

There are many different betting structures under which Omaha is played. Betting structures can be categorized as limit, pot-limit or no-limit. In the United States, most Omaha games are played with fixed limits, as I'll explain in a moment. In Europe, most Omaha games and other poker games are played as pot-limit. There are also several hybrid structures, in which high Omaha betting is limited before the flop, played pot-limit after the flop, and played no-limit after the last two rounds.

Limit or fixed-limit Omaha means that the permissible amount of each bet on any given betting round is pre-established. In American casinos, limit Omaha and high-low Omaha stakes are most often described by two numbers, such as $5/$10 or $10/$20. The first number prescribes the fixed amount of all bets and raises during the first two rounds of betting; the second number prescribes the amount of all bets and raises during the last two rounds of betting. Thus, unless a player has less money on the table than required (and hence must go **all-in**—wager everything he has), the amount of each bet or raise is fixed at the prescribed amount.

For example, in a typical ten-handed $10/$20 Omaha game, the first two players to the dealer's left will each have posted blinds. The first player on the dealer's left posts the **small blind** of $5 (a half bet), and the player two seats from the dealer posts the **big blind** of $10 (a unit bet). The first person to act voluntarily is the *third* player to the dealer's left. That player may call the $10 unit bet, raise $10, for a $20 total wager, or fold. Again, all bets and raises in a $10/$20 game made during the first two rounds of betting are in increments of $10. All bets and raises made during the last two rounds of betting, after the fourth and fifth board cards, are in increments of $20.

# 2 BASIC STRATEGY AND CONCEPTS

## UNDERSTANDING OMAHA HIGH-LOW

To understand Omaha high-low, first you must realize that there is a big difference between loose Omaha high-low and tight-aggressive Omaha high-low. Most of the Omaha high-low games that you encounter are loose to very loose and are usually played for lower stakes, roughly $10/$20 or lower. One quantitative measure of a loose game is whether more than five players on average are seeing the flop. (See "Cappelletti's Rule," later in this chapter for further explanation.)

Tight-aggressive Omaha high-low is usually played for higher stakes, often $30/$60 and higher, and is often the big game at casinos with many tables in play. These games often seem more like tight hold 'em. They incorporate "hard serve and rush the net" tactics, rather than loose, multi-player, happy-go-lucky Omaha high-low.

At tight-aggressive Omaha high-low, frequent raises before the flop often narrow the field to one or two callers and the blinds. Thus, on average, well under four players see the flop. At tight Omaha high-low, it is fashionable to play very aggressively to keep the pressure on your opponents.

Because of its **shorthanded** nature, with fewer players in any given pot, tight-aggressive Omaha high-low tends to emphasize interpersonal poker battles. At loose multi-handed Omaha high-low, it is usually you against the field, and you can peacefully sit back, go with the flow, and build the pot opportunely.

In order to gain a thorough understanding of what kind of hands win at the two extremes of Omaha high-low, and some games in the middle, it certainly helps to delineate the various types of starting hands and to analyze their strengths and weaknesses. I will discuss starting hands in the next section; for now, it is sufficient to describe this subject more generally.

At loose Omaha high-low, you will probably show a profit if you play only starting hands with an A 2, A 3, some 2 3 hands, and very good high hands. Some hands with an A 4 or A 5 suited and some other good holdings are better than marginal in most loose games.

At tight Omaha high-low, your favorite raise-before-the-flop hand is a pair of aces with one or two low cards. Aces play very well against one or two opponents. Your next favorite hand is an ace with a 2 or 3 suited and one or two working high cards. But note that A 2 or A 3 and two other low cards plays much better against three or more opponents than it does when the game is shorthanded.

At tight Omaha high-low, I frequently see good players raising early with an ace and three low cards or high-only cards. Since both of those hand types win more at full-table play—four or more players—it is wrong to raise early and narrow the field with such hands. It is better to smooth call and try to draw in extra players.

One-way high hands—four cards 9 or higher—are most profitable when there is just one or no low cards in the flop and a number of now worthless low-card hands have built a large initial pot.

It is important to understand that you must evaluate carefully your starting hand both before and after the flop. If a before-the-flop raiser usually has an A 2 holding, that information is valuable when you're deciding how to play your cards. If a late before-the-flop raise builds an unusually large starting pot, it is often correct to raise bullishly after the flop or crawl in on marginal cards, if you can do so cheaply. Note that the round of betting after a flop with two or more low cards is often even more active than after the flop at hold 'em.

One of the big secrets to winning in all Omaha high-low games is not to waste money on hands which have become liabilities. Fold them. The players who most consistently have large stacks of chips in front of them are usually players who participate in the fewest hands and often fold after the flop. You'll notice that they are very aggressive in the hands they do pursue.

Finally, for evaluating your own expectations at Omaha high-low, note that an expert's edge over the good players at Omaha high-low is not nearly as significant as it is at hold 'em, high Omaha or seven-stud. The bottom line is that a good-medium Omaha high-low player can win almost as much as an expert in a loose Omaha high-low game! If you happen to be a good player, why struggle for skinny profits at hold 'em? Find yourself a nice plump Omaha high-low game, averaging five-way action or better, and have some fun also.

## BASIC STRATEGY FOR OMAHA HIGH-LOW

An old friend who has played very little poker over the past ten years asked me what he should know to play Omaha high-low (8 or lower). After making the usual disparaging remarks, I assured him that the basic strategy is simple and surprisingly uniform—that is, it applies to almost all loose games with mostly multi-handed pots at low levels. Very tight, aggressive games, in which most hands are three-handed or head-to-head duels, have a somewhat different almost hold 'em-like basic strategy.

Basic strategy for Omaha high-low starts you out correctly and certainly gives you an appreciable advantage over typical loose players. Of course, there is no substitute for experience to recognize the several hundred specific tactical situations for which there are varying strategies depending on the number and type of opponents.

Basic strategy for Omaha high-low should either include or be prefaced by several statements or warnings to advise the prospective player of certain objectives and pitfalls. The first warning is to remind you to avoid the deadly triangle! Beware of competitive situations where a lock-high and a lock-low will raise you to death. In many typical Omaha games, though, a lock-low simply will call in fear of being drawn and quartered—split low and receiving merely one-quarter or one-sixth of the pot—or in fear of non-locks folding a raise.

Perhaps the best general advice is to gear your play towards **scooping,** winning whole pots. It is difficult to win at high-low if you win only occasional half-pots. Your overall game plan should be to sit back patiently and wait for big hands with whole-pot potential. It is wise to avoid dubious hands with only half-pot potential, where you risk more money than you win.

A simple basic strategy for Omaha high-low is as follows:

**1.** Play only very good starting hands, especially in early seats. *Very good* means hands containing low cards, especially an A 2. Almost any hand containing an A 3 is also playable. Hands containing a 2 3 need some additional values. Ace-high flush couples with a 4 or a 5 are marginal hands. Most other low hands are for suckers. Very good high hands are mainly those with all four cards 9 or above, or those which have fourteen points or more. (See my point count system in Chapter 6). Avoid "high" hands with medium cards, 6s through 8s—which also make lows.

**2.** Do not get involved after the flop without primary nut potential. A **nut** hand is one in which you have the best possible hand. Do not call with only a non-nut draw in a two-way pot, especially if there are raises. If you are going to play after the flop, *play very aggressively* with **pushing** hands, ones in which you have good potential in one direction (that's why you are still playing), and marginal potential in the other direction.

**3.** Play conservatively after the turn except for occasional bluffs in high-only situations. Avoid getting **squeezed**, paying multiple double bets, with second-best cards. Be lucky on the river!

## OMAHA HIGH-LOW HAND TYPES
Continuing with our difficult quest to understand Omaha high-low, let us focus on ten types of marginal or better starting hands and examine their strengths and weaknesses. Keep in mind that all hands are better when suited or double-suited.

| Hand Type | Example |
|---|---|
| **1. Pocket aces with** | |
|     **a.** two prime low cards | A A 2 4 |
|     **b.** one prime low card | A A 3 10 |
|     **c.** two low cards | A A 5 7 |
| | |
| **2. A 2 with** | |
|     **a.** two low cards | A 2 5 7 |
|     **b.** one low card & one high card | A 2 6 K |
|     **c.** two high cards | A 2 Q J |

**3. A 3 with**

      **a.** two low cards                    A 3 5 7

      **b.** one low card & one high card     A 3 6 10

      **c.** two working high cards        A 3 K♥ J♥

**4. A 4 5 with**

      **a.** low card                       A 4 5 8

      **b.** high card                     A 4 5 Q

**5. 2 3 with**

      **a.** 4 or 5 and low card          2 3 5 7

      **b.** high pair                   2 3 Q Q

      **c.** 4 or 5 and king-suited      2 3 5♥ K♥

      **a.** two working high cards     2 3 J K

**6. Ace-suited with 4 or 5
and two high cards**                A♥ Q♥ 10 4

**7. Pocket aces and two high cards**     A A Q 10

**8. Four high cards (9 or higher)**     A Q J 10

**9. High pocket pair and
two prime low cards**             Q Q♥ 4♥ 2

**10. "Low bags" such as
    2 4 4 5, 3 4 4 5, 3 4 5 6, etc.**     2 4 4 5

Some things to keep in mind on the ten high-low hand types as listed above:

**1.a.** When pocket aces are accompanied by very low cards and/or ace-other flush draws, you want more players in the pot to increase the payoff when you hit "the nuts." In an early seat, do not raise before the flop (that tends to lessen attendance).

**1.c.** Pocket aces and medium low cards are both most effective in shorthanded play; hence they constitute two reasons to raise before the flop to lessen attendance. When you have pocket aces, the fewer opponents you have, the greater your prospects of winning high without improvement. Medium-low cards are more likely to win low when there is less low competition (the "emergency low" often saves you half a pot).

**2.a., 3.a., 4.a., 5.a.** Hands with four low cards are not as profitable as some people think, since low is usually a struggle and there is less chance of backing into high. Note that although a holding of A 2 and two other low cards plays very well multihanded, it is not much of a favorite at head-to-head, if at all. Thus you should *not* raise with this type of hand before the flop if the raise narrows the competition.

**2.b.c., 3.b.c., 4.b., 5.b.c.d., 6.** Having a good low draw with one or two high cards, often with an ace kicker, gives you some two-way prospects if, in addition to a nut (or second nut) low draw, you also match a high card in the flop. Bet and raise very aggressively with fragile bidirectional holdings, especially if promotion is likely.

**7.** Pocket aces with two high cards, unlike most high only hands, should raise before the flop if the raise rates to reduce the field to one or two players, as it does when you're in a tight game. But note that whenever the flop contains two or three low cards, most high-only hands are anti-percentage liabilities, especially if a low card shows on the fourth card.

**8.** Four high cards (9 and higher) are highly flop dependent since they are cost-effective only when there is no more than one low card in the flop. On high-only flops, these hands get excellent odds because the starting pot has been enlarged by low-oriented hands that must now fold or play at great disadvantage.

**9.** "High pair plus" is playable only in very loose games in late position.

**10.** Most of these hands are not playable at a profit in most games (by mere mortals). Even after most good flops they are drawing for second or third best hands.

## HEAD-TO-HEAD OMAHA HIGH-LOW

In the last section we discussed ten types of Omaha high-low starting hands. What happens when these various hands end up head-to-head against each other? Some of the following results might surprise you and affect your shorthanded strategy.

The most significant overall fact, as I have pointed out in previous books, is that in Omaha high-low, it is very rare for one hand to be more than a two-to-one favorite against another hand. More than likely, at head-to-head, the hand that raises before the flop is less than a 60% to 40% favorite against the defending hand. Thus, the big blind should defend quite liberally, especially in all-in situations.

It is critical to understand that there are some hands that play poorly against many opponents but play much better shorthanded or at head-to-head. Thus, in a tight Omaha game in a late seat you frequently raise before the flop to narrow the field or steal the blinds with an ace and medium-low cards. The following data suggests that it is probably correct to do so also with a middle pocket pair and proximate cards (such as 6 6 5 4), especially when your cards are double-suited. Low flush cards are also more valuable shorthanded!

The following table gives the percentages of the hand on the left winning against the other six.

| Hand | 1 | 2 | 3 | 4 | 5 | 6 | 7 |
|------|------|------|------|------|------|------|------|
| 1. A A 5 10 | - | 59.6 | 65.5 | 62.3 | 60.1 | 70.6 | 59.4 |
| 2. A 2 5 7 | 40.4 | - | 46.6 | 55.1 | 61.8 | 56.7 | 58.9 |
| 3. 8 8 6 4 | 34.5 | 53.4 | - | 51.6 | 57.4 | 52.7 | 58.8 |
| 4. J 9 3 2 | 37.7 | 44.9 | 48.4 | - | 57.6 | 46.9 | 52.8 |
| 5. 5 4 3 2 | 39.9 | 38.2 | 42.6 | 42.4 | - | 53.7 | 47.8 |
| 6. K J Q Q | 29.4 | 43.3 | 47.3 | 53.1 | 46.3 | - | 44.6 |
| 7. 9 8 7 6 | 40.6 | 41.1 | 41.2 | 47.2 | 52.2 | 55.4 | - |

Note that pocket aces are always a favorite at head-to-head, especially when they're suited and with one or two low cards. Pocket kings are often an underdog at head-to-head, unless they're with two low cards.

A fine hand for multihanded play, such as A 2 5 7 or A 2 3 4, usually loses slightly at head-to-head to a medium pair and proximate low cards. Acey-deucey hands are drawing hands two ways, you want to draw in more opponents to increase the odds on your draw.

Good high card hands are most profitable multihanded when a high flop trashes the low hands that contributed to make a healthy starting pot. But at head-to-head, good high card hands are usually an underdog to any random hand with several low cards.

Finally, note that medium wraps are not good hands at Omaha high-low, either multihanded or head-to-head.

They're not low enough to win against other lows, and good, high flops with 8s, 7s, and 6s usually result in split pots.

## STARTING HANDS AT HIGH-LOW

I have long held that the optimum strategy for starting hand selection at Omaha is relative to the game in which you are playing. Given your playing skills, image, and position, you can expect to show a long-run profit by playing starting hands which are some degree better in quality than the hands being played by your opponents. But just how much better? One of the most significant areas of skill in Omaha high-low is in determining generally where to draw the line and then optimizing by making small adjustments.

The looser the game, the greater the payoff potential of any winning hand, and the more marginal starting hands that will show a profit in the long run. If a hand rates to show a profit in the long run, you probably should play it, unless you prefer to avoid the greater swings incurred by playing marginal hands.

Is there an easy way to judge or quantify the average quality of the starting hands being played by your opponents? Yes! You can categorize a table fairly accurately by observing the average number of callers before the flop. Here's my rule for choosing an Omaha table: If an average of five or more players are seeing the flop (including blinds), or if several players frequently chase after the flop, then you have found a home. With eleven tight players, an average of less than four players would see each flop. So if the average number of callers is five or more, you know that some losing cards are being played. If the average is well above five, then you have indeed found a home!

It must be that the world is having difficulty adapting to Omaha, because most Omaha high-low games I encounter are "rule games"—they satisfy my rule of having five or more callers before the flop. In these loose games, I recommend calling to see the flop from any position with the following starting hands: good high hands (fifteen points or more using my point count system in Chapter 6) preferably with all four cards 9 or higher; two-way hands containing an A 2, A 3, some 2 3 hands, and certain mixed hands.

Note that if all eleven players used this same formula, only 3.8 players on average would see each flop, two blinds plus 1.8 per nine hands. You might opt to call with certain mixed hands, such as ace-other flush couple with high cards and a 4 or a 5. Just which 2 3 hands can be played profitably requires some explanation. I will discuss it later in this chapter. In very loose, friendly games, you might relax these requirements slightly, especially when you're in late position. Position is more important with two or three high-card flops.

A quick warning: the above recommendations do not apply to tight, often big-money, Omaha high-low games where fewer than four players on average see the flop. When most players either fold or raise, hands frequently become head-to-head duels and are often a two-way chase with one of the blinds. Those situations more resemble hold 'em than the loose Omaha high-low we all know and love.

Relativity tells us that in tighter games, the profitability line shifts to better starting hands. **Polar** hands which emphasize high with high pairs (especially aces), and high cards with an A 2 or A 3 are best, but low serves more as your back-up in these hands. Against few callers, low-oriented hands (A 2, A 3, and other low cards) are less valuable since winning only the low half of the pot usually nets less than you have invested. Many of the lesser A 3 hands which are profitable in a loose game are not profitable in tight competition. Even some A 2 hands are not profitable, especially when someone has raised. I have seen very few of these tight Omaha high-low games on the East Coast, although the occasional $15/$30 and $20/$40 games sometimes tighten up a bit.

I usually categorize hold 'em games as very loose, loose, tough, or tight, and my categorizations usually reflect increasing stakes. But there really are only two categories of Omaha high-low: loose and other! And there is little incentive to play in the second category. A class hold 'em player has a big edge over medium-to-good players and does well in tough or tight games. But because of the vagaries of bi-directionality, the luck factor at Omaha high-low is greatly increased, and the expert has less edge over the average good players.

The most significant skill differential at loose Omaha high-low occurs between the fish and any player who knows enough to play only good percentage hands. That alone constitutes such a huge mathematical advantage that in most typically loose Omaha high-low "rule" games (games with five or more callers before the flop), a good Omaha player might average as much per hour as a good hold 'em player at twice the stakes, with the benefit of less variance and downside.

After years of experience and careful consideration, I feel that, even leaving some room for error, I know what can be played profitably at loose Omaha high-low. Actually, my formula for winning at loose Omaha high-low is a bit conservative. You may relax it somewhat in wild games.

Note that in rule games, much of your edge and expected profit comes from loose opponents playing bad starting cards. Since that advantage vanishes or lessens considerably at tight and shorthanded Omaha high-low, you may choose to avoid games where it is not profitable to play all A 2s and A 3s.

Some very selective professional hold 'em players use this same concept when they follow this rule: *avoid playing in hold 'em games where playing ace-jack in first seat is not profitable.* This rule applies to many higher level hold 'em games.

Loose Omaha high-low is fun to play, and with a relatively simple formula, it becomes a very good "working man's" game. And Omaholics seem to be increasing in number rapidly.

It certainly seems that most Omaha high-low games, at least, those that I have encountered, are generally loose with an average of five or more players seeing the flop.

I recommend that in these loose Omaha high-low games, all four-card starting hands containing an A 2 or A 3 are playable. That is, seeing the flop with these hands rates to show a profit in the long run. So what about the next best low holding, a 2 3? I know several good Omaha high-low players who routinely play all hands with a 2 and a 3.

Note that a 2 3 generally requires finding an ace and at least one other low card (not a 2 or 3) on the flop to be playable after the flop, just as the A 3 holding tends to require a deuce on the flop. But an A 3 is considerably better than a 2 3, not only because the A 3 is lower, but also because the ace has great high potential, especially when it's combined with other related cards.

So is the low potential of the 2 3 sufficient to make any four-card starting hand containing a 2 3 playable? My opinion, a clear "no," although there are some exceptions in loose games and in late positions.

Let's look a little closer at playing a "bad 2 3" hand. As I noted earlier, in order to have a good low flop, a 2 3 has to flop an ace with at least one other low card, not a 2 or 3. Then it needs yet a third low card on the board (one of sixteen **outs**—cards that help your hand) to complete the nut low, and no 2 or 3 **bust card**, a card which would counterfeit the 2 or 3 in your hand. Computer simulations indicate that when you hold a 2 3 and two high cards, the five board cards will contain an ace, no 2 or 3, and at least two other 8 or lower cards about 13% of the time. Note that an A 2 makes the nut low with three or more low board cards and no ace or 2 about 24% of the time. If you like flop statistics, a 2 3 flops a nut low or draw—an ace, at least one other low card, and no 2 or 3—about 13% of the time. Note that an A 2 flops a nut low or draw about 36% of the time.

Even when your 2 3 makes a nut low holding, you usually get only half the pot—unless, of course, there are one or more other 2 3s lurking, in which case you usually lose money with only one-fourth or one-sixth of the pot. Even when you win half of the pot, you usually do not make a large profit. If four players call all the way to the showdown, you win only an amount of money equal to the amount you invested plus half the "dead" money from the callers who dropped out early.

The salient concept here is that although your 2 3 has good low potential, you simply cannot get rich at Omaha high-low if you're playing for low only. Your Plan A should be to play cards with good prospects of winning the whole pot. Winning only low should be more of a fallback plan—Plan B.

Thus, if your 2 3 is accompanied by two unrelated and unimpressive cards, for example, an unsuited king and a 9, seeing the flop with such cards will most likely make you lose money in the long run. You are more likely to make money playing a 2 3 if your hand also contains something extra, such as two proximate high cards, preferably suited, a pair, or other low cards, preferably a 4 or a 5, to improve your two-way chances. Since your 2 3 prefers an ace on the board, you need some cards that can beat the aces over high holdings.

The following percentages may give you a better feel for the low potential of the best two-card low holdings ("low couples"). These percentages are based on the frequency of the indicated low couple (with two other cards 9 or higher) winning low against five other random hands that play until the showdown. Note that the degenerative "trips-in-hand" variation (2 3 3 3) has better low potential due to less frequent "busting" and fewer ties (but it has very little high potential).

|         | % Low Wins | Wins | Losses | Ties |
|---------|-----------:|-----:|-------:|-----:|
| A 2     | 3.9        | 19.8 | 8.0    | 8.2  |
| A 3     | 20.1       | 16.6 | 11.4   | 7.0  |
| 2 3     | 17.7       | 14.5 | 14.0   | 6.4  |
| A 4     | 16.7       | 13.8 | 15.2   | 5.8  |
| 2 4     | 14.7       | 12.0 | 17.1   | 5.4  |
| 3 4     | 13.0       | 10.6 | 18.7   | 4.8  |
| A 2 2 2 | 29.3       | 27.5 | 4.9    | 3.6  |
| 2 3 3 3 | 24.0       | 22.5 | 10.2   | 3.0  |

In my opinion, the bottom line is that you should not play a bad 2 3 even in a typically loose Omaha high-low game. Although a 2 3 does have substantial low potential (it's valued at about 6 or 7 points in my point count system, see chapter 6—depending on position), unless you are playing in a very high pay-off game, a hand featuring a 2 3 needs a bit more substance to be playable. And, as always, whenever you are playing a marginal holding, you strongly prefer to be acting in late position.

## OMAHA HIGH-LOW FLOP TYPES

A three-card flop can have zero, one, two, or three low cards (8 or lower). At Omaha high-low split, it is intriguing how much your after-the-flop strategy can change depending on the number of low cards in the flop. It's almost like playing four entirely different games.

What percent of the time do three cards contain zero, one, two, or three different low cards? Answer, 5.1%, 32%, 46.6% and 16.2% respectively. But if you are holding a typical good Omaha high-low starting hand with three low cards and one high card, for example, A 2 4 Q, then taking those cards out of the deck changes the percentages by about one-percent to 5.6%, 33.1%, 46% and 15.3%. If you hold four high cards (9s through kings), you will flop zero or one low cards, a high flop, about 30% of the time (3.2%+26.9%).

The following brief discussions of the four flop types indicate four entirely different strategic directions:

### High

If all three flop cards are 9s through kings, obviously there can be no low; hence you are playing high Omaha. However, there usually is a much bigger starting pot than there would have been at straight high Omaha because of the contributions from low-oriented hands which would not have seen the flop at straight high. Note that even at most loose Omaha high-low tables, there are normally more low-oriented hands being played than high-card hands. Thus, in these situations, high-card values are worth much more than at straight Omaha high.

Because many of the low-oriented hands will fold, creating very favorable odds, you should usually join in the hunt (call, bet, or raise) with any reasonable prospects for high. Fierce competition from aggressive players (often with scant values) can cause huge swings but they add to your profit in the long run. In an aggressive game, trapping is often profitable, and you need not fear opening the door for the lows by checking it out. And bluffing is quite fashionable on high-only hands.

### Highish (one low card)

With only one low card in the flop, low only hands get bad odds (low makes about one time in five; a nut low draw makes one time in six). But a good (two-card) low draw is a significant addition to any combination hand or marginal high holding. Percentages favor betting liberally, especially in late positions and especially in a tight game with fewer chasers. Since late-acting hands strain to bet, to get the low competition out before seeing a low fourth card, and perhaps steal the relatively large antes or go one-on-one, with a good high hand in early position you might opt to trap and check-raise if there are perpetually aggressive players downstream.

### Lowish (two low cards)

Two low cards on the flop, which occur almost half of the time, devalue and portend likely problems for the high hands, since low will make well over half of the time. Note that vigorous raising at after-the-flop rates will not keep out the nut low draws, but it will certainly put big pressure on second-nut or worse one-way draws. Since good high hands, combination hands (marginal or better both ways), and bad players all like to raise after the flop, there is often a lot of action. Note that nut low draws have no reason to raise—except perhaps to promote high holdings. But a third-nut low draw, with a playable high holding, should venture a raise to squeeze second-nut draw low-only hands (see "Promo Raises" in Chapter 4).

## Low

When the flop contains three low cards, there will be one or more lows sharing the pot, and there is often much betting. Since the highest hand will be taking only half the pot, all high only holdings must be seriously devalued! Even the best high hands are highly subject to danger and abuse. Even a nut flush draw (absent other potential) is often not worth pursuing if you win high roughly 25% of the time, especially when there is very aggressive betting. Even high sets (trips) are subject to lows free rolling, since the last two cards will pair the board only about one-third of the time, whereas the last card frequently makes a possible straight, which is held roughly one-third of the time (depending on the number of players).

Unbreakable lows generally **pull**, encourage others to bet, but they are sometimes torn between pulling more players in and pushing out weak high competition. In most super-nut low situations, including draws, the quality of your high potential dictates your push/pull strategy.

Next time you play Omaha high-low, notice how often the number of low cards in the flop completely changes your perspective of a hand.

## "CAPPELLETTI'S RULE"

Over the years, I have received numerous correspondences and comments about what the "Cappelletti's Rule" is, a term coined by some of my poker friends in 1992—not by me. The original rule identified a loose and favorable Omaha game, where an average of more than six players are seeing the flop. Several years later, I revised that number to *more than five*. Thus, an explanation is in order.

In the early nineties, I made various recommendations about seeking out Omaha games where two-thirds of the players were seeing the flop. At that time, it was merely an instinctive recommendation. On general principles, we all know that a game cannot be bad if two-thirds of the players are seeing the flop!

Some time later, around 1993, I performed computer simulations, described below, which indicated that in a ten player game with two blinds, about 80% of the time, only two of the eight voluntary players would hold adequate four-card starting hands. What are adequate before-the-flop starting hands at Omaha high-low? The above-mentioned computer program dealt out eight (or nine) four-card hands and then checked each hand for an A 2, A 3, 2 3 or all four cards 9 or higher, a simplified version of the criteria suggested in my original book, the 1989 *Cappelletti on Omaha*.

If two or fewer of the eight players held adequate starting hands about 80% of the time, there should be four or fewer players (adding two blinds) in about eighty percent of the hands. If five or more players on average are seeing the flops, then one player or more, again on average, is playing an inadequate starting hand. That fact alone should indicate that a good player should be able to show a profit in that game, especially if the one or more players who are playing loosely are also playing somewhat loosely *after* the flop as is usually the case.

Note that my computer program counted all 2 3 hands. Although you might consider playing many 2 3 hands in a very loose game or when you have reason to get involved with marginal cards, most good Omaha high-low players consider fewer than half of all 2 3 hands to be adequate starting hands. For example, most 2 3 hands with a 9 are dubious at best.

Since my program counted all 2 3 hands, the numbers in the following table are a bit high. But that overage roughly compensates for a few very specific hands which my program did not check for but which most experts would play, such as ace-suited with a 4 and a 5.

The following profiles indicate how often zero, one, two, three, and four or more adequate four-card starting hands were counted in 100,000 deals (eight-hand deals as in a ten-handed game, and 100,000 nine-hand deals as in an eleven-handed game):

| # found in 8 hands | | # found in 9 hands | |
|---|---|---|---|
| 0 | 11.0% | 0 | 7.8% |
| 1 | 33.8% | 1 | 29.1% |
| 2 | 35.4% | 2 | 36.6% |
| 3 | 16.1% | 3 | 20.4% |
| 4+ | 3.8% | 4+ | 6.1% |

If you add up the percentages for zero, one, and two players for eight voluntary players, as in a ten-handed game, the total is 80.2%. Similarly the total for nine players, as in an eleven-handed game, is 73.5%. So most of the time, two players or fewer have adequate starting cards. Thus the average number of callers before the flop in a ten- or eleven- handed Omaha high-low game should be fewer than four, even if both blinds always play.

If an average of more than five players are calling before the flop, it's a good sign that at least minimally profitable conditions exist in that particular Omaha high-low game. It is a mathematical indication that there is money to be had.

To put this discussion another way, a good player should show a long-run profit in that game. We would all certainly prefer to play in Omaha high-low games where more players on average were seeing the flop, but probably "more than five" is the minimum criterion you should use to identify a potentially profitable game.

Note that when you play in a game with a before-the-flop average well under five, that game is not loose. You can no longer expect to make money simply on mathematics; too many players are doing the same thing. In these situations, the whole character of the game changes, and you often find yourself in tight-aggressive one-on-one dogfights, which somewhat resemble hold 'em. Tight Omaha high-low, often at higher stakes, is an entirely different game.

## HAND POWER RATINGS AT HIGH-LOW

In November of 1995, I introduced the concept of **hand power,** a method of quantifying starting hands for both hold 'em and Omaha. Hand power indicates the approximate frequency of a given hand winning compared to a random, average hand. For example, against four opponents, a total of five players, a random hand rates to win 20% of the time. A hand with a 1.5 hand power therefore rates to win about 30% of the time (1.5 x 20%).

Applying this hand power method, which is essentially a weighted average combining the results of three computer runs for each given hand against seven players, three players, and one player, to Omaha high-low (8 or better) starting hands yields the following interesting results:

## HAND POWER RATINGS FOR SOME OMAHA HIGH-LOW HANDS

| | | | |
|---|---|---|---|
| A 2 A 3 | 2.18 | 2 3 9 8 | .93 |
| A 2 A 3 | 1.86 | 2 3 5 J | 1.08 |
| A A 3 Q | 1.53 | 2 3 4 5 | 1.24 |
| A 9 A 5 | 1.43 | 3 4 5 6 | 1.04 |
| | | 4 5 6 7 | .86 |
| A 2 3 4 | 1.77 | 5 6 7 8 | .76 |
| A 2 3 4 | 1.60 | 2 4 6 8 | .93 |
| A 2 3 10 | 1.54 | | |
| A 2 K Q | 1.52 | A 4 Q 10 | 1.33 |
| | | A 4 Q 10 | 1.17 |
| A 2 9 8 | 1.34 | A K A K | 1.44 |
| A 2 9 8 | 1.16 | K Q Q 10 | 1.08 |
| A 3 9 8 | 1.09 | Q J J 10 | 1.06 |
| A 3 10 8 | 1.14 | A Q K J | 1.15 |
| A 3 10 7 | 1.17 | Q 10 J 9 | 1.04 |
| A 3 9 7 | 1.10 | Q J 10 9 | .86 |
| A 4 9 8 | 1.00 | A 10 Q 9 | 1.08 |
| A 4 9 8 | 1.16 | A Q 10 9 | .83 |

Two underlined cards are of the same suit. Note that the nut-flush couple (ace-other) increases hand power by about .17, one-sixth times average win rate. Note also the relatively low hand power of most high hands. The hand power for most high hands at Omaha high-low is about 30% less than the same hand at straight high Omaha.

As I mentioned, hand power is based on computer simulations. In these simulations, all players stay in until the showdown, which ignores the realities of betting after the flop. Wrap hands and high-card hands that hit a high flop and then bet, folding hands that might have improved on the last two cards, probably do better in real life than in computer simulations. Hands which are connected or concentrated are more likely to yield multiple prospects with good flops. They allow for aggressive post-flop pot building and bigger payoffs, which thus increases their actual worth.

Note also that when you play a big one-way high hand at high-low, if you hit the flop with two or more high cards (not aces), most of the low hands fold or play at a disadvantage and the initial pot size is often more than double what it would have been had you been playing straight high. That fact obviously increases the value of high hands on high flops. However, a low fourth card, making a board with two low cards, can make the high hand harder to win. It generally reduces your expectations.

The value of all high hands decreases considerably on over half of the flops when there are two or more low cards present. Sometimes aggressive post-flop betting by those pesky lows can even drive out a high hand which would have been a winner with typical straight high betting.

Although most wrap and big high-card hands are probably more valuable than the above hand power ratings indicate, I nevertheless feel that there certainly is a message here. One-way high-card hands simply do not have the overall winning potential found in the premium low hands, which are actually two-way hands. In real life, scooping a two-way pot is usually much more lucrative than winning a straight high pot. The bottom line is that, though there are some tactical and psychological exceptions, at Omaha high-low, generally, you should play only one-way high hands with hands which would be good enough to raise before the flop playing straight high Omaha.

## FREQUENCY OF OMAHA HIGH-LOW STARTING HANDS

Many players ask exactly which starting hands they should play at Omaha high-low in early seat and in late seat, and how often they should pick up such hands. Note that it is easier to give precise answers to these questions for Omaha high-low than for hold 'em.

Since having more cards makes it more likely that a **lock**—unbeatable hand—is present, position is somewhat less important in Omaha high-low than in hold 'em. Hence, there are fewer default pot situations, where no one has a good hand. At Omaha high-low, the bi-directionality makes betting inferences more ambiguous. Although it is clearly advantageous to sit in late position with hands that have flopped well, the overall advantages of late position at Omaha do not affect your starting hand requirements as drastically as in hold 'em. Thus, at Omaha, there is significantly less spread between early and late seat starting hand requirements than at hold 'em.

I have often recommended playing only conservative Omaha high-low starting hands, namely, low hands with an A 2 or A 3, some hands with a 2 3, and high hands evaluated at fourteen or fifteen points or higher using my point-count system, see Chapter 6. These are all hands which would be good enough to raise before the flop at straight high Omaha. How often do you pick up these hands?

You are dealt any two-card combination—such as an A 2—about 6.4% of the time. You are dealt a three-card combination—such as A 2 3 (often called "ABC")—about 1% of the time. If you play all A 2 and A 3 holdings, except when you hold three-of-a kind, and more than half of the 2 3 holdings, then you are dealt one of these playable low hands about 15% of the time (approximately 5.4+1+5.4+3.2).

If, in addition to the 15% low hands, you play good high hands with fourteen Cappelletti points or more, you will be adding about 17% additional high hands, not counting high hands which were already included in the 15% low hands. If you prefer playing only fifteen or more point high hands, you would be adding about 13% additional hands. I usually play a little less than a third of the hands in early seat. That is about 30% of the hands. In later positions you can loosen up a bit.

In addition to the above-mentioned hands, there are some "mixed" hands, mostly those with an ace-suited, a 4 or a 5, and two other good cards (two high cards, a high pair or touching low cards). Such hands usually have a hand power rating of about 1.3 and can be played profitably, especially from later seats, and especially in looser games.

Most of the above recommendations assume you are playing in a game of average quality, with at least one or two **fish**, weak players that make for easy pickings. Note: There is very little incentive to play Omaha high-low in a game without any fish. If you happen to find a wonderful game in which many players are playing every hand and giving away money, you can profitably play some lesser high and mixed hands, especially from later seats.

## PRIMARY VALUES AT HIGH-LOW

At Omaha high-low, most of the time it is right to be very conservative and voluntarily play only *primary* values both before and after the flop. Understanding what constitutes a primary holding after the flop should help you recognize which primary holdings are worthwhile before the flop.

A **primary holding** after the flop is either a strong high hand or a draw (namely a full house or higher, nut flush, high nut straight, trips, nut-flush draw, high two pair or eight-outs-or-more *high* nut straight draw) or a nut low or nut low draw.

A primary before-the-flop holding consists of two cards which will yield a primary after-the-flop holding fairly frequently, let's say more than 10% of the time. The primary before-the-flop two-card holdings which most frequently result in after-the-flop primary holdings are A 2, A 3, and 2 3 with low flops, and A A, K K, Q Q, AX suited, and four working high cards (preferably all 9 or higher) with high flops. Since almost all worthwhile starting hands at Omaha high-low contain at least one of these primary holdings, you should have second thoughts about playing a hand without one.

Note that even though most one-way high hands get poor computer ratings at high-low, four-high-card high hands nevertheless have ample value when there is a high flop (fewer than two low cards) since there is more money in the starting pot than there would be in a straight-high pot (that is, money put in by low hands) and less high competition.

Good secondary before-the-flop holdings are not usually playable by themselves, but they are often playable in combination with additional prospects. Examples of good secondary holdings are high-medium pairs (jacks through 9s), KX suited, touching high cards (for nut straight draws with high flops), and any two cards 5 or lower.

Secondary holdings, which have some value, but quite often just cost you money, are pairs of 8s through deuces, QX and all lower flush holdings, and all other low cards. Note that secondary and lesser two-card holdings often flop combinations which seem playable and sometimes win, but you probably have noticed that they have a high mortality rate. For example, after-the-flop low straight draws are very bad investments by themselves, but they can be very valuable when played in combination with other prospects.

At Omaha high-low, most of the giant pots that you win come from hands where you started with primary values.

When you play a starting hand containing multiple primary values, you are more likely to flop multi-dimensional two-way potential. One reason *not* to play less-than-premium starting cards is that when you "hit the flop," it is usually a one-way hit. One-way hands lose much of their value in a two-way pot! When you start with a premium hand, quite often Plan B or Plan C saves the day after Plan A fails. Obviously, hands without a "Plan B" are much less likely to back into half or sometimes all of the pot!

To put this another way, when you play a hand without depth, even if you flop a playable one-way holding, your overall prospects are usually not much better than marginal, when you are playing for only half a pot. Much of the time you are essentially playing to protect money already invested or you have only a small positive expectation. Most speculative actions with lesser cards at high-low are generally marginal, that is a small positive expectation in the long run, and are mostly important for image and future payoff prospects. Those who regularly play mediocre starting hands are often "unlucky" and seldom realize why they are long-run losers, even when they compete correctly after the flop). To be a long-run winner at Omaha high-low you must keep percentages on your side by playing primary values.

## MARGINALITY

At some point on the road to enlightenment and to mastering Omaha high-low strategy, you should become aware that there are some very interesting options for marginal hands. Many marginal starting hands at Omaha high-low can be played with a long-run expectation of very little profit or loss. But just which marginal hands can be played at a slight profit is highly game dependent.

Why play "nothing" hands? Mostly to adjust your image. In most loose Omaha high-low situations, you want to be loved more than feared, so to speak. Also, perhaps you want to inject a little fun and fish-camaraderie into the game. At Omaha high-low, it is certainly prudent to display occasional imprudence. Again, though, it all depends on the overall looseness and other players in the game.

Many 2 3, A 4 and A 5 starting hands are borderline or worse, even at loose Omaha high-low and again this depends greatly on the game. Paradoxically, some of these hands actually play better at tight, shorthanded Omaha high-low (A♥ K♦ 7♠ 5♠). When you play marginal starting hands, it is important to fold most of these hands after the flop. But although you strongly prefer primary holdings to get involved after the flop, sometimes a lack of interest in betting by the other players indicates an opportunity to divvy up the antes.

To sharpen your perspective, study the following typical marginal situation. You are playing A♥ 6♥ 4♣ 10♠ and flop 7♥ 9♦ 3♠. Although you have the second nut low (a deuce would give you the nut low), and an 8 or a 5 will give you a straight—but both non-nut—note well that this is the kind of hand you would rather have an opponent play while you draw to your usual prime A 2 plus. In five or six-way action, the A 2 holding rates to make more than twice as much money as the A♥ 6♥ 4♣ 10♠ holding.

But if the betting gets checked around to you, you should make a speculative bet to fold some opponents and improve your chances for high. After several checks, the odds change somewhat, and it's now about 50-50 that there is an A 2 present. Note well that making this lead bet after the flop should not commit you to sticking around after the fourth card (when the betting doubles). Whenever you find yourself fishing along with a marginal hand, be prepared to fold on the turn if raising occurs or is likely.

Similarly, when you've seen the flop on A♥ 5♥ 4♦ 5♦—one of the best hands without an A 2 or A 3—let's say you flop A♦ K♦ 8♠. Clearly your low and little flush draw are marginal holdings. But if it gets checked around to you or just the person in front of you bets, you might try a bet or a raise. If you manage to narrow the action to one or two opponents, you would probably be in a "marginal plus" situation.

Again, do not lose sight of the fact that you would much prefer to be pushing primary holdings, such as a 2 3 with a higher flush draw, in which case your money expectation would be more than double your present holding. In the long run, you will show only a small profit playing these marginal hands.

Without a doubt, playing marginal hands after the flop is an art form. And sometimes the basic underlying mathematics are actually negative. I have often discussed certain advantages gained by aggressive raising after the flop. But even against weak and loose players, it is unsound to "over push" against a substantial mathematical disadvantage. So what if you do?

A classic two-way marginal-minus example is holding a 2 3, perhaps K♦ 2♦ 3♠ Q♣, when a 4 5 6 hits the flop. In a ten-handed game, you will be losing low to an A 2 or A 3 about 75% of the time, although a "promo" raise—see Chapter 4—after the flop might fold a prudent A 3. And clearly your ignorant end straight is a favorite to lose high even if it happens to be high at that moment after the flop. But the combined odds of losing both ways are at least close to marginal against only one or two loose opponents.

Even though the underlying mathematics are dubious, in a five- or six-way pot, *if* it gets checked around to a loose player on your right who bets, it might work out well if you raise! Understand that I am not recommending this as a sound, money-making play. But if your raise narrows the field to two- or three-way action, you might show a slight profit depending on the looseness of your one or two opponents. If either player is super-solid and rates to have one-way locked up, your expectation would certainly be minus.

Step back and take a look at the overall big picture. If you do fish in to the end and get beat both ways, make a big splash so that everyone at the table sees your hand and realizes that you are loose as a goose, and perhaps not as good as they thought. If you are playing in familiar company, it is a good investment occasionally to turn over "bad cards." Some players do it all the time. And sometimes the bad cards win.

In general, at Omaha high-low, it is occasionally a good investment occasionally to "go beserk" and make a super-aggressive raise, especially after the flop with a two-way marginal hand. If one extra caller pays you off on a subsequent hand, you get your investment back—with the "good will" as ample interest.

It is sound advice to expend most of your speculation budget just after the flop. If things do not look promising, give it up. Do not throw good money after bad. If your play after the flop is significantly better than that of the average player in the game, you should show a slight long-run profit when you play these marginal hands, especially if you play them only occasionally. Understand that the big long-run pay off, in most games, is the PR or advertising value which can significantly affect how well you are paid off on many of your big hands if your opponents love to call you.

## OMAHA HIGH-LOW: THE BOTTOM LINE
Most of the Omaha high low poker games spread in casinos are of the loose variety, especially those at lower stakes,

$10/$20 and below. There are very few tight aggressive Omaha high low games. In tight aggressive Omaha high low, there is usually one or more raises before the flop and only one or two callers (often the big blind). In loose Omaha high low, there is extra money in most pots, which means that the better hands will show extra profit in the long run.

Is Omaha high low a very skillful form of poker? Quite the contrary! Loose players love Omaha high low because unlike hold 'em, they can play almost any hand and have some chance of winning half of the pot. And since in Omaha high low there are often huge pots and cruel last-card swings, on a lucky night, even the worst players will find themselves scooping up large stacks of chips.

Many poker experts turn up their noses at Omaha high low because it has such a high luck factor. And most Omaha high low experts realize that because of the bi-directionality, their edge over good medium level players is rather thin. But both experts and medium level Omaha high low players have a considerable edge over the weaker players. Thus, one main reason why Omaha high low is becoming so popular with both experts and the vast population of medium players is because the bottom line hourly win rate is considerably better than at hold 'em.

It is widely accepted that the average hourly win by a good player in an average hold 'em game is about one and a half big bets per hour. That is, a good player should win on average about $30 per hour in an average $10/$20 hold 'em game. It has been my experience that in a typically loose Omaha high low game, the good players win an average of about two-and-a-half to three big bets per hour, that is, almost twice as much per hour as in hold 'em. Can this be true?

Note that a substantial part of your hourly winnings in Omaha high low comes from playing hands with an ace-deuce or an ace-three, although there are many other hands which can be played with a positive expectation. You pick up an ace-deuce or ace-three (in your four hand cards) more than once a round, roughly once in eight hands. How often does an ace-deuce or ace-three win? According to computer simulations (for example, Caro's Poker Probe), both ace-deuce and ace-three hands win over one fifth of the total pot money when playing against seven random opponents. But in the simulation, all eight hands are played to showdown. In real life, some of the simulated hands would fold because of the betting, and sometimes fold what might have been the winning high or low hand. Because your ace-deuce or ace-trey often keeps you in the pot, your hand will actually win considerably more often than in the simulations, probably about 30% of the total pot money, depends somewhat on the game—but more likely to be greater than 30%.

The average Omaha high low pot size varies greatly —depending mainly on the looseness of the game. Although five or six players might see the flop, the average numbers of players at showdown usually averages less than four. The average pot size in hands which a tight player participates, will probably exceed 21 small bets. Note that even without any raises, three-and-a-half callers to showdown would put 6+6+6+3 unit bets into a pot. Thus, with other callers before the flop and possible raises, 21 bets is certainly not an excessive estimate. And if super-large pots are occurring more frequently than occasionally, the average pot size might be closer to 30.

If there are roughly 32 hands played per hour at your table, then on the four ace-deuce or ace-three hands that you play in an hour, you should gross about 30% of the 84 total chips in the four pots (4 x 21) or about 25 chips per hour. Subtracting about 13 chips invested or lost (typically 6+4+2+1 or less if you often fold after the flop; if you have invested a lot more, then you probably have won more than 25), and 6 chips for four sets of blinds in one hour, leaves a net profit of about 6 unit chips per hour which is three big bets per hour. And again, this is playing only your ace-deuce and ace-three hands.

If you can manage to show a profit on the other hands that you play, so much the better. If you sit back and play high percentage hands, your chances of winning in the long run are much better than the house's winning edge in the various casino games, such as blackjack, craps and roulette. Your bottom line is in your own hands.

What else do you need to know to get started? Most simply stated, the basic strategy for winning at Omaha high low is to play only good starting hands, continue after the flop only with high percentage holdings and not to get caught with losing cards in big betting on the last two rounds at double the bets. If you are pleasantly surprised with your results, remember that "almost anyone can win at Omaha high-low."

# 3 | BEFORE THE FLOP

As is true for most forms of poker, no single aspect of your strategy determines your ultimate fate as a winner or loser at Omaha more than your initial calling strategy. At Omaha, there seems to be a universal tendency to enter the pot with less than adequate hands. With more people staying in the pot, there is more ensuing action. This, perhaps, is one reason for the popularity of Omaha high-low.

Recently, I played at a relatively loose and lively table of nine players where they alternated one round of hold 'em and one round of Omaha high-low. It was unusual to get more than five flop callers at hold 'em, but it was also unusual to have fewer than seven flop callers at Omaha! At Omaha, family pots, in which everyone calls, were common.

Why is Omaha generally looser than hold 'em? Simply because, as you may have guessed, the difference in winning potential between the best and the worst initial four-card hand in Omaha is much less than in most other poker games. For example, a player who regularly fishes in at hold 'em with two random cards wins much less frequently than does an Omaha fish calling with four random cards. Why does the Omaha fish win more often? Because four cards make six two-card combinations, each equivalent to a two-card hold 'em hand, so there are many more fourth street and last card turnarounds.

Thus, a good Omaha player must think in terms of the pluses and minuses of all four cards. To think about just your best two-card combination, or even your two best two-card combinations, is like playing pool without using the rails. When you have several long-shot combinations, in addition to your main holdings, they often add as much as five or ten percent to your overall winning potential. It is usually very difficult to compute the actual mathematical value of all your two-card combinations at the table. But many of the best Omaha players develop their judgment and perhaps intuition so that they reevaluate various positions using these secondary considerations.

## SPECULATING AT HIGH-LOW

Recently I was asked if any four low cards (8 or lower) are adequate to get involved before the flop at Omaha high-low. If the four low cards do not include an A 2, A 3, or 2 3, my general answer is simply "No," or "Not recommended." The negative response is particularly strong if the four cards do not include an ace. Note that even the 6 5 4 3 smooth wrap fails to win an adequate percentage of hands to be considered a good call.

For nomenclature purposes, let's call the above hand—that is, any four unpaired low cards (8 or lower) and not including an A 2, A 3 or, 2 3—a **low mixed bag**, since at Omaha, the term **mixed bag** indicates four cards without prime couples that work together sufficiently to be playable or almost playable. A **prime couple** at high Omaha is a two-card holding consisting of either a high pair or two suited cards J 10 or higher (and worth 6 points or more in my point-count system on Chapter 6). Although a low mixed bag hand is not a good call at Omaha high-low, it is playable as an occasional speculative hand. What is a speculative hand?

In most games, there are times that one departs from basic strategy or percentage plays for psychological reasons or other considerations. In gin rummy, for example, you normally pick up only cards that complete a three-card meld. But occasionally you speculate by picking up a card that fits well with several other cards in your hand. And very rarely, experts sometimes pick up a card as a red herring, more to confuse the opponent than to be useful.

In contract bridge, you sometimes make a blatantly inadequate bid, called a *psyche* or *psychic bid* to confuse the opponents and perhaps steal a suit or elicit a favorable opening lead.

In seven-card stud, you sometimes call or raise even if your first three cards do not contain a pair or three good cards.

In hold 'em, you sometimes call or raise, especially in late position, with dubious hands like 5 4 suited. Calling or raising with that sort of hand in hold 'em is somewhat analogous to playing mixed bag hands in Omaha high-low.

One of the main reasons for this sort of speculating is to confuse your opponents as to your playing style. Thus, whenever you get caught playing such a hand, do whatever is necessary, including skillful theatrics, to get all the thinking players to notice. Consider it part of your advertising budget.

Keep in mind that when you play speculative hands, you are basically bucking sound percentages. In high-low Omaha, especially when the going gets rough, there is no substitute for having the nuts. With low mixed bag hands, you seldom have the nuts. Thus, with these hands, you will have to back down if you're challenged. Surprise and your expert skill at reading situations, which is tough at high-low, are your main advantages.

On the positive side, I should note that in real life Omaha, a fairly large percentage of pots and half pots are won with not-so-good hands—hands that are certainly less than the nuts. When the dealer forces you to take the chips, it does not matter what your hand was. But, if your style is aggressively to seek out many of these opportunities (as opposed to merely recognizing those that come along when you are playing sound cards), you are probably playing too loose. You're likely costing yourself money—unless you are very lucky or playing in an unusually weak game.

However, when the conditions are right—and even the greatest experts have some difficulty recognizing such at high-low—it is sound strategy *occasionally* to "step out of line" and play an off-beat hand—such as a low mixed bag. You can expect a good flop about 20% of the time, and a marginal flop (with approximate break-even odds) an additional 10% of the time. With 6 5 4 3 and A 7 5 4, the percentage of good flops is slightly higher.

In a tight game, if you raise before the flop with one of these hands in late seat, your plan is to bet a high flop if it is checked around to you. Depending on what happens, you might decide to follow through on an outright bluff.

Thus, in high-low Omaha, even though you normally require an A 2, A 3, or 2 3 to get involved with low cards, occasionally you might speculate with a mixed bag of low cards in late position. It helps keep the game honest. I cannot emphasize strongly enough, though, that this sort of speculation is sound and successful only if done *occasionally*.

## HIGH-PAIR-PLUS-LOW HANDS

Once, when I played in a $5/$10 Omaha high-low game with a kill, fate dealt me two rather rare "high-pair-plus-low" hands, which I consider marginally playable. Understand that high pocket pair hands are not usually playable at Omaha high-low, that is, profitable in the long run, unless they're accompanied by other 9-or-higher high cards or two great low cards.

If you run a computer simulation with pocket kings and two random cards against five random opponent hands, the pocket kings hand wins only about 17.4% of the time (16.7% is average). For comparison, if you ran a simulation with an unsuited A 2 and two random cards against five random opponent hands, the A 2 hand would win about 26.8% of the time. But when a high pocket pair is accompanied by two prime low cards, 5 or under, *and* it's double-suited, the total potential is at least marginally playable in most loose games.

First I held pocket kings double-suited with a 4 and a deuce, which I know from experience to be playable. If you simulated playing that hand against five random hands, the K 4 K 2 wins about 25.3% of the time (16.7% is average), an A 2 hand wins about 26.8% of the time.

Several nights later, I picked up pocket queens double-suited, also with a 4 and a deuce, which I believe is playable in most games. Note that pocket queens being less valuable than pocket kings is much less significant than queen-high flushes being more dangerous than king-high flushes. If simulated against five random hands, the Q 4 Q 2 wins about 23.3% of the time.

I made money with both hands. With the pocket kings, I ended up with a nut high flush when the A♠ came on the river. Unfortunately, the ace was the third low card, which cost me half the pot.

The pocket queens hand flopped K♦ 3♣ Q♣. I raised with my set and then reraised, but there was still five-way action, unusual attendance for a high flop! Fourth street brought the 7♣! Not only was there now a likely flush out against me, but the spirited after-the-flop betting might even have meant that someone had pocket kings. There was a bet and a raise, and I would have folded if I hadn't had a reasonable low draw also. I called confidently in four-way action and no one reraised.

An 8 hit the river. There was a bet, a fold, and a raise to me. But this raiser was known for his pressure betting. The rough odds of someone holding either A 2 or A 4 initially were about 70%. But with only one low card in the flop and spirited betting, a player with an A 2 or A 4 might have folded unless he also had working high cards. So I braved it out and called with my backdoor low, knowing well that my trip queens were now probably worthless.

Luckily, the raiser was in fact trying to promote a bad low (which went along with his bad flush), so I backed into half of the large pot. None of us like to be in these "fish in" situations, but they're all part of the game in Omaha high-low. Note that it is usually unwise to get involved in a call down in a situation where you might have to put in three or four double bets unless you have good reason to do so.

Also note that if the betting after the last card had been a bet by the fourth-round raiser—presumably on the big flush, and a call, I might well have considered raising with my third-nut backdoor low (depending on the caller's propensities).

All in all, these rare high-pair-plus-low hands, especially when double-suited, seem to be at least marginal, maybe better.

## DO FIGURES LIE?

There's an old saying, "Liars figure but figures don't lie." But figures derived from computer poker simulations do not always represent real-life poker situations.

A computer-literate Omaholic recently asked me whether I would rather have K J J 9 or J J 5 2 (again, the underline represents suited cards) as an Omaha high-low starting hand. I responded with the usual chapter, book, and verse that I usually play most four-cards 9 or higher in games where an average of more than five players see the flop, and that I would not play J J 5 2 except to defend my blind.

He then proudly presented me with a computer printout which compared the above two hands when simulated against one, two, three, and five random opponents, as well as simulations with Q Q 10 9 versus Q Q 5 2. In all of his simulations, the pocket pair with the 5 and 2 won a higher percentage of hands than the same pair and same flush draw with the two high cards. That's interesting, but not necessarily significant.

First, note that his simulations were against totally random opponent hands. In real life, at least one and usually more of your opponents is seeing the flop with a hand that includes an A 2 or A 3. Using Mike Caro's Poker Probe, I reran his sixteen simulations, but I specified that one of the opponent hands would contain an ace and a 3, which, in my opinion, makes the simulations more realistic.

The results given in the following table, with just one opponent starting with an A 3, closed the gap between the pair with 5 2 and pair with high cards by several percentage points. In the simulation with five opponents, the pair with high cards actually performed slightly better than the pair with 5 2.

| | 5 opponents | 3 opp | 2 opp | 1 opp |
|---|---|---|---|---|
| K J J 9 | 17.64%* | 24.45% | 31.85% | 1.89% |
| J J 5 2 | 17.20%* | 25.17% | 32.80% | 6.72% |
| Q Q 10 9 | 18.72% | 26.01% | 32.22% | 43.0% |
| Q Q 5 2 | 18.48% | 26.58% | 34.27% | 7.92% |

* In his simulation without an A 3 hand against five opponents,

the K J J 9 won 16.1% of the time, and the J J 5 2 won 18.2% of the time.

Even though the above simulations seem to indicate that the 5 2 hands win more than the high-card hands, that does not necessarily correspond to more money in your pockets. The main reason to play four high cards is that when you get a high flop, one with two or three high cards, you rate to have much better odds of winning than you do with the various low-oriented hands. It seems likely that in a high-flop situation, the two extra high cards would be more useful and provide a better Plan B in winning the pot than two low cards. It is also likely that some of the 5 2 simulation wins are of the back door low or back-in variety, which, in real life, would have been folded after the flop.

Notwithstanding that the percentage figures from his simulations tend to indicate that the mixed hands win more often than the four high-card hands, I do not recommend playing those hands, except perhaps occasionally in very loose company. But Q Q 4 2 double-suited might be good enough to play in late seat.

In running the above-mentioned simulations, I noticed that the hand with the A 3 and two random cards always won 10% more than the other hands. Now those are figures which I do believe. And that's where I prefer to put my money.

## RAISING WITH ACE 2 SUITED

I once wrote an article in which I mentioned that I had raised on the button playing loose Omaha high with an A 2 suited. A reader e-mailed to ask if I always raise in late seat with an A 2 in loose Omaha high-low.

My answer was that you can probably make a case for raising in late seat with any A 2 whenever there have been numerous callers. But I like raising in late seat with an A 2 if the ace is suited or with any other good high holding, simply because this could be the *big one* that I have been waiting for and I would like to make it bigger.

By raising on the button, not only do I double the size of the starting pot, but the big starting pot also tends to keep more players in after the flop. If I manage to **scoop**, win both high and low, just one of these big pots in a three-hour session, I rate to finish comfortably ahead.

Note that when you hold an ace-suited, deuce, and any two other cards, you will hit a good playable flop about half of the time, a playable flop is conservatively defined as having an already made hand or having a multiple-card draw for the nut low or nut high.

To get a better feel for hitting the flop with an ace-suited and a deuce, I recommend you try the following simple exercise:

Take the ace and deuce of spades out of a normal deck of cards along with two other not-so-good cards, for example, a 7 and a jack. Then deal out the other forty-eight cards into sixteen flops (16 x 3 = 48). Notice that usually five or six of the sixteen flops have two or three low cards without an ace or deuce. One or two flops will contain two or three spades. And one or two flops will have some good high holding. Thus, usually eight or higher flops are clearly playable.

In addition to the clearly playable flops, you will notice that there are often other flops which you would play if you could get in cheaply after the flop—when no one raises. For example, with a combination hand flop with a gut ace-high straight draw, one spade, and one low card, it would certainly be cost-effective to see the fourth card for a single bet.

Are there any negative aspects in raising? Does it hurt your chances of winning the pot if too many other players hang on tenaciously because the pot is large? It might affect your chances of backing into high with a lesser hand.

But having lots of callers certainly fits in well with your main plan, namely, drawing for, or already having the nuts. If you hit, you would like to have as many callers as possible especially if they stick around and pay you off on the last two double-bet-size rounds.

One possible negative consequence of raising too frequently on your button might occur if one or more fish notice that you raise frequently on your button. If they become more selective on your button because they fear you might raise, that would certainly cost you money.

Note that in a ten-handed game, when you have an A 2, there is about a 36% chance that one or more other players also has an A 2. That possibility of getting quartered is one of the strongest arguments against raising with an A 2 and little else.

Of course, in addition to the above, there are several other variables—the inherent speed of the game, often gauged by the frequency of before-the-flop raises, your judgment of the capabilities of the fish in your game, and your Omaha image—which influence your optimum raising strategy.

Also keep in mind the fundamental concept of playing Omaha: it is better to be loved than feared. Most formulas for success in loose Omaha high-low are based on getting as many callers as possible. Thus, in normal loose Omaha playing environments, you will probably get more callers by keeping your raising demeanor affable and unintimidating.

## PLAYING AGAINST AN A 2

I once was playing in a $10/$20 Omaha high-low game at the Taj in Atlantic City. After several hours I had noticed that the player three seats to my right had raised before the flop seven or eight times, and each of the times that we were able to see his raising hand, he had held an A 2. And he had raised with his A 2 holdings both in early and late positions. And he had *not* raised before the flop when holding pocket aces under the gun.

On my little blind, I picked up an unimpressive 10 6 4 2 with two hearts. In middle seat, that same opponent raised before the flop, and his raise was folded around to me. Since there were good chances that I knew half of his hand, I raised, hoping to get the big blind out. The big blind folded, which left just the two of us. Was my assumed knowledge of his hand a sufficient advantage to justify playing a mixed junk hand?

On the flop came the Q♥, 9♥, and a 3. Pretty useless except for the flush draw. But it probably looked bad to my opponent also. Since I probably knew two of his cards, he rated to have only a pair at best. Note that having the flush draw, which would probably win high if it hit (and it hits about one time in three), provided additional justification for playing the hand aggressively.

I thought about betting. But that might get him into calling mode. I had watched him stubbornly call down other opponents on two prior occasions. So I went with the two-way check to either get a free card or bluff a check-raise. Note that the two-way check is a ploy that I use more frequently after the turn card in hold 'em.

He bet. I check-raised. I had a tight image, and I knew he didn't like it. But he called. If he was capable of putting me on a hand, he probably thought I had top two pair or trips.

The turn card was the 5♦, which was actually a good card for me. It gave me seventeen outs for a straight. But even more important, if my opponent made his low and hence would call my next bet, then every low-making card but an 8 would give me a straight for probably half of the pot, and an ace or deuce would probably give me a scoop. Obviously I had to bet to preserve my illusion of a high hand in case the river card was a high card. In that case I would have to bet, since he might well fold, and that would be my only chance of winning.

The last card was a 10. So there was no low. I thought about betting, but he might well call if he had my just-formed pair of 10s beat. And now that I had this pair of 10s, I no longer had to make the desperation bet to make his ace-high card fold (which prior to my pair of 10s, would have beat my no-pair hand if we both checked at the showdown.

So I checked. He thought a moment and checked also. He had a 9, which gave him a pair of 9s, along with his expected A 2. My pair of 10s won the pot. Another game of inches.

So the operation was successful, and the patient even lived. But if, instead of the 10, some other high card had hit the river, it is not clear whether he would have called my bet with only a pair of 9s. The bottom line is that sometimes, even in wild and woolly Omaha high-low, you can acquire very valuable information about opponents' tendencies, and it often provides a basis for various later maneuvers. Having information which is probably accurate at Omaha high-low is often sufficient to prevail against what might otherwise be superior cards.

## DUPLICATION
One interesting but annoying situation in Omaha high-low occurs when you are holding a nice low-oriented hand but

then there are several raises before the flop in front of you by normally tight players. How valuable are your low cards if several other players are looking at the same low cards? What if only one other player seems to have the same cards as you?

Let's say you're playing $10/$20 Omaha high-low. You finally pick up a hand containing an A 2, but without another prime low card, 3, 4, or 5. For example, say you pick up an A 2 7 J of four different suits. The tight player to your right, who normally plays only very good hands, raises before the flop. That's only the second time he has raised before the flop in two hours. His previous raise was based on an ABC (A 2 3) holding. What do you think of your hand?

We all agree that an A 2 is the best two-card holding in Omaha high-low (with the possible exception of aces in certain tight games) and normally any hand with an A 2 rates to show a profit in the long run. But if another player also has an A 2 and a better overall hand than you do, for example, he has another prime low card, then even if your A 2 makes the nut low, you will probably be playing for a quarter of the pot!

If you knew for sure that your opponent had duplicated your A 2, you would have a clear fold with a lesser A 2 hand, such as A 2 7 J unsuited, because you rate to lose money if you play it! And surely you should not reraise, though some do!

If you run a computer simulation with four players in which one hand has A 2 7 J unsuited, the second hand has A 2 4 and a random fourth card, and the other two hands are random, the A 2 4 hand wins about 29% of the time (25% is average), the two random hands each win slightly less than 25% of the time, and the lesser A 2 hand (A 2 7 J) wins only about 21% of the time.

Extending that simulation to six players with four random hands and eight players with six random hands really demonstrates the value of having another prime low card in addition to the ace and deuce. With six players, the A 2 4 hand wins about 23% of the time, the four random hands each win about 15.5% of the time, and the A 2 7 J hand wins only 14.3% of the time. With eight players, the A 2 4 hand wins over 19% of the time (12.5% is average), the six random hands each win 11.3% of the time, and the A 2 7 J hand wins 11.5% of the time.

Although the above simulation is by no means conclusive, I believe that it does tend to show that when more than one hand holds an A 2, it seriously reduces the winning potential of that holding. It also clearly emphasizes the great value of holding an additional prime low card.

So it all boils down to just how likely is it that the before the flop raiser has actually duplicated your A 2. Many very tight players raise before the flop only with A 2 plus something else such as a 3 or a 4 holding or perhaps pocket aces plus. It would really help if you had happened to notice how the raiser had played pocket aces previously. For example, if you noticed that he had played several pocket aces holdings by merely calling before the flop, then the chances of his holding an A 2 would be significantly higher. Of course, an A 2 hand might well be profitable, especially with a lot of players, if the other two cards have better than average high potential and/or if the ace is suited.

I realize it is very disappointing when you have been patiently waiting for a nice hand, and you finally catch an A 2, to then have to throw it away. I've folded a not-so-hot A 2 holding after a tight player's before-the-flop raise about a dozen times in the last few years, and every time I have saved money.

# A CLOSER LOOK AT A 4

A conservative approach to loose Omaha high-low is to play only starting hands containing an A 2 or A 3, some hands with a 2 3, or very good high-card hands, preferably high-card hands with all four cards 9 or higher. My definition of "loose" Omaha high-low is a game in which an average of more than four players is seeing the flops. Note well that tight Omaha high-low, usually for higher stakes, where roughly three players see each flop, is an entirely different game.

At loose Omaha high-low, in addition to those hands mentioned above, there are other starting hands that rate to make money. In very loose games, some winning players play many hands that contain an ace-suited, especially when they're in late seat. It has been my experience that in most loose games, playing starting hands with an ace-suited and a 4 is clearly better than marginal, especially in a late seat. But, in order to make money with an A 4 holding, you should keep in mind some important qualifications. If you choose to get involved after the flop with marginal two-way holdings (that is, marginal in both directions), you should play very aggressively to narrow the action. Even more importantly, you must often fold these hands when the going gets rough.

Let's take a closer look at the somewhat dubious low prospects of an A 4 after the flop. The only time you really like the flop for low is when a 2 *and* a 3 flop—without an ace or a 4. That happens only about one time in thirty. If neither a 2 *nor* a 3 hits the flop, your low prospects are simply not playable by themselves. An A 2, A 3, or 2 3 will be lurking about 86% of the time with nine opponents and 90% of the time with ten. Note that even minimal low prospects might contribute enough to make marginal high prospects playable. And, indeed, this Omaha concept that several less than playable holdings can add up to a playable holding often applies to playing an A 4 with high prospects.

If a two *or* a three and another low card, not an ace or 4, flops, your A 4 is in exactly the same position as a player with an A 3 when the flop contains two or three low cards that are 4 or higher. And, as with that classic A 3 situation, you must be intensely aware that your second best holding can cost you big bucks. In a ten- or eleven-handed game, the chances that the nut low draw is actually held against you are about 50-50. (Assuming that any A 2 and A 3 starting hand is always played, the nut low draw will be held in an eleven-handed game about 53% of the time and in ten-handed game about 49% of the time).

Should you bet on the flop in late seat with second-nut low draw? Normally, you should not bet the second-nut low draw by itself, but you should bet if you have some marginal or better high prospects also. Without high prospects, your first preference would be to draw for your miracle one card nut low cheaply. And you would also prefer to keep the stakes low while you see what happens if one of the three other low cards hits the turn. That would give you the second-best low, since there are eight low cards, you are looking at four, and the other four make a low. When you have the second-best low, it is critical to judge from who bets and who calls or raises whether you must fold your second-best hand. If you have no high prospects, you often fold, depending on who is in the pot and betting. At best, you rate to win only half a pot or less. *Never lose sight of your main objective at high-low: to win the whole pot.*

Since an A 4 is more likely to be valuable after all five cards have hit the table than just after the flop, having marginal high prospects after the flop often justifies seeing the fourth card if it's cheap. But marginal two-way values strongly suggest an aggressive tactical approach. If the betting gets checked around to you and you also have some high prospects in addition to your second nut low draw, then the fact that it's seldom wrong to bet the flop when many others check around to you. Your bet might take the antes or put you one-on-one or up against fish chasers, with hands worse than yours both ways.

Conservative poker players often have trouble digesting the principle that a substantial two-way promotional effect occurs if you raise aggressively after the flop. Facing possible expensive action, many otherwise playable one-way hands *and* two-way marginal hands—like yours, but you "got there first," so to speak—must, or at least should, fold because of the inadequate pay-off of a half- or quarter-pot win. When the field can be sufficiently narrowed, quite often one mediocre two-way marginal hand will show a profit by backing into the direction that is not locked up. And it sometimes wins the entire pot with a lucky last card. And backing into half or whole pots is good for your "trash-man" image. Remember, in Omaha, unlike in hold 'em, it is better to be loved than feared.

Summarily, when you play an A 4 hand, you will seldom flop a miracle nut low or nut low draw. Much more frequently, you will find yourself in a second-best low situation with marginal high prospects also. These are swing hands that many prudent players prefer to avoid. I, too, avoid these hands whenever a locksmith (rock) type leads the betting after the flop. If a rock is betting, at least one-way is spoken for. I like these hands much better when I am the bettor or raiser in friendly company. But, and here's a warning: when you play second-nut cards, and opponents raise, you should get out of the pot.

## PROMO RAISES BEFORE THE FLOP

The well-known promotion raises after the flop in Omaha and Omaha high-low can be very effective (see Chapter 4), and that same kind of aggressive thinking has been extended to certain before-the-flop situations.

A **promo raise** is a raise made with lesser holdings, sometimes called *third-class holdings* in order to intimidate an opponent with slightly better *second-class* holdings and pressure him into folding. When you make a promo raise, you're accepting the calculated risk of encountering the best holdings, *first-class holdings*. The totality of promoting the relative worth of your holdings, plus promoting your positional advantage by causing downstream players to fold, plus grabbing the initiative, including bluffing options, and gaining future advertising value often makes the promo raise a worthwhile action.

Some of the holdings in high Omaha which promote well with early-seat raises before the flop, that is, play better against less competition, are high pairs without good draws, low flush couples, and, to a lesser extent, low straight holdings. In loose games, where a raise before the flop does not seriously reduce competition, this whole concept simply does not apply.

Note the principle that prime draw holdings like ace-other flush couples and high cards *should* prefer more competition, which usually results in greater pay-off odds. Similarly, in Omaha high-low, the A 2 holding should prefer more players because of better pay-off odds and occasional all-the-way fish, for example, with A 3. Hence, the prime holdings should not normally make early seat raises; those tend to lessen competition.

Be aware that the original promo raise was made with the third-best low, a 2 3, to represent holding an A 2. Its holder wanted to shake up and make his opponent fold with the second-best low, A 3. If it doesn't work before the flop, you can try a promo raise again after it. Similarly, a classic high Omaha gimmick raise was with the queen-high flush, after a three-of-a-suit flop, which might make king-high fold.

Once upon a time, when raising before the flop on any A 2 was fashionable, a savvy A 3 holder lived in fear of raised pots and getting sucked in because pot was large. Now that enlightened Omaha players often do not raise before the flop with A 2 holdings in early positions—except as a variance—an early seat before the flop raise is more likely based on a good high hand, or it is indeed a promo raise. But A 3 holders must always live in fear of the potential big disaster—unless, of course, a 2 hits the board.

Thus, with certain hands containing a 2 3 or A 4 and some attractive other high holdings for example, a high pair, it is often correct to make an early promo raise (as a cat-and-mouse effort suggesting A 2) to lessen second-rate competition and promote your low chances. When you've raised before the flop, if the flop contains two low cards 4 or higher, you might follow through with an after-the-flop promo raise, though obviously this is sounder if you have good high prospects also. Bold speculation after the flop often wins especially if done only occasionally, but, of course, all speculative hands must yield to any pressure after the fourth card when the bets double.

Let's say you're playing Omaha high-low (8 or better), and you pick up 2 3 4 7 double-suited in first seat. This is not really a good hand unless you flop an ace and another low card, and that happens fewer than one out of six times. However, in last seat the odds might be revised based on the number of callers before the flop. You might make the classic two-way promo raise with these cards—if you are playing in a game where there are players who are good enough to fold raises.

Not only might you fold a timid A 3 empty, you might also fold some higher flush draws. If you get a lot of callers, you will need a good flop though you are less likely to flop an ace. Against only a few callers, your hand may play very well while your raise improves your chances of bluffing high and winning with a low flush. Note also that with few callers, a 2 3 is more likely to flop an ace.

In modern Omaha high-low, promo raises have become very fashionable, and they're often made quite indiscriminately. And reverse psychology and strategy are becoming more prevalent. Unfortunately for expert players, all this makes Omaha high-low more random and harder to read than ever. And more dangerous equals less edge. It's good news, though, for various types of medium level players who can play Omaha high-low at a slight plus (assuming that there are some fish in the game), and who now get some of the plus money previously won by the best players. Perhaps that is one reason why Omaha high-low is steadily gaining popularity.

## DEFENDING YOUR BLIND AT HIGH-LOW
Let's say you're playing $50/$100 Omaha high-low. On your $50 big blind you pick up 9♠ 7♠ 4♦ 2♦.

First of all, remember that this game is *not* a typical loose Omaha high-low game in which five or more players call to see the flop. These higher stakes Omaha high-low games seldom have well-attended pots. Frequently there is a raise before the flop, and most players fold. In that way it resembles high stakes hold 'em.

As usual, one of your seven opponents raises before the flop—he's a rather tight player—and it gets folded around to you. Because you have three low cards, and because the two-double suits add over 7% to your expectations, you decide to defend head-to-head.

If your opponent is raising on an ace and one or more other prime low cards, most likely, an A 2 holding, and if you were going to play the hand out to the end, this particular blind hand would win the confrontation about 40%-45% of the time.

But, although you would win 40%+ of the time if you played the hand to completion, and you will win this confrontation less than one-third of the time because you often have to fold after seeing the flop. In making the critical decision to continue after the flop, you should be aware that a tight before-the-flop raiser often has an A 2 holding or pocket aces. A 2s occur almost three times as often as pocket aces.

This time, in real life, I happened to hit a good flop, 8♠ 5♠ 3♥. I had a flush draw and meshed well with the low cards while my opponent might have counterfeited his 3. But note that if my opponent did have an A 2, then I was still an underdog. According to Caro's Poker Probe, my expectation would be about 45%.

Since I was acting first, I saw no reason to bet this low flop. My opponent surely would. I checked, he bet, and I called. There was now $325 in the pot. The Q♠ hit the turn, which gave me a flush. I checked, and he bet the $100. Should I then have raised?

I don't think so. Although at that point I was fairly likely to win at least half the pot, my judgment was that I was more likely to lose the whole pot than to win the whole pot. I figure it was rather likely that he had either an A 2 or an A 4, which meant I would need an ace on the last card to win low. And my low flush was a long way from being the nuts—he might even hit a full boat on the last card.

So I just called. The river card was another queen. I checked and feared the worst. He bet. I called. He had the A 2 low, and he did have a queen for trip queens. And his ace was the A♠. But, fortunately, he did not have another pair to make a full house, and he did not have a second spade, so my little flush salvaged half of the pot. I had risked losing $350 and I ended up winning $12.50.

I couldn't help noting to myself that I had what looked to me like a decent blind-defending hand, I hit a good flop, I hit my flush, and I still needed luck to break even. Maybe there is a message here about defending your blind with mediocre cards.

Which of the following flops would you play with the hand 9 7 4 2?

| | |
|---|---|
| 1. 8 <u>7 6</u> | 6. Q♠ 10♠ J (note four flush) |
| 2. 5 4 3 | 7. <u>J</u> 10 <u>8</u> |
| 3. 8 6 3 | 8. 10 <u>6 5</u> |
| 4. J 7 5 | 9. K 5 3 |
| 5. A 10 9 | 10. A 6 3 |

Possible Answers: Take a look below. The first number is the percent of the time that the 9 7 4 2 wins against an ace, deuce and two random cards; the second number is the percent of the time that your hand wins against the actual opponent's hand, A 2 Q 10. (Both percentages were calculated using Caro's Poker Probe.)

| 1. 40% 48% | 6. 50% 42% |
|---|---|
| 2. 15 % 32% | 7. 78% 58% |
| 3. 32% 41% | 8. 35% 33% |
| 4. 38% 47% | 9. 28% 33% |
| 5. 30% 24% | 10. 52% 60% |

You are a favorite with flops 7 and 10. You should fold flop 5. You would have a negative return if you play hands 2, 3, 8, or 9 against an opponent who probably has an A 2 though you might be a favorite against a lunatic. On hand 6, a high flop with flush draw, you should bet on the flop if there is any significant chance that opponent might fold. Flops 1 and 4 are marginal. Here, again, your opponent's style is a prime consideration.

# HIGH LOW BLIND DEFENSE IN A TIGHT AGGRESSIVE GAME

Playing six-handed tight aggressive $25/$50 Omaha high low, a much different game than the usual loose Omaha high low. On my big blind, I picked up the nine and four of diamonds and the eight and three of hearts. A rather aggressive player raised it to fifty before the flop, which was all folded around to me. Would you defend your blind with my cards?

In the early nineties when I was working with various Omaha high-low computer analyses, in order to determine whether or not a computer-simulated player should defend its blind with a not-so-good starting hand, I formulated, the following "blind-calling point count" approach (not to be confused with my Cappelletti Point Count for Omaha high starting hands). Obviously you would also defend your blind by calling or raising if you had a good starting hand, that is, a normal Omaha high low calling hand, for example, a hand containing an ace-deuce or ace-three or four high cards nine or higher.

## Big Blind Head-to-Head vs.
## Before-The-Flop Raiser

2 points  any two prime (ace-five) low cards
1 point  3rd low card (eight or lower)
1 point  4th low card (eight or lower)
2 points  pocket pair nines or higher
1 point  pocket pair eights or lower
1 point  two cards of the same suit
1 point  two cards touching or once removed ("one hole")
1 point  an ace

If you have a not-so-good four-card starting hand which adds up to five or more of the above points, tests have indicated that there will be more than enough high-low winning potential to show a long-run profit defending your big blind. In a recent article, I pointed out that another factor in defending your blind was whether or not the before-the-flop raiser would tend to pay you off (having betting momentum) when you hit.

Since the given hand (9-8-4-3) contained seven of the above points, even though I didn't particularly like the hand, I chose to defend. "Think red," I thought to myself. The flop came king and six of hearts and the seven of clubs. Not great, but it gave me a flush draw (albeit low—but OK for head-to-head), a two-way straight draw and a not-so-good low draw. For low, I would have much preferred an ace or deuce in the flop.

I checked to him and he bet as expected. I called. Note that I was now rooting for the ace or deuce of hearts or a five or ten straight card. The nine of spades turned, somewhat counterfeiting my nut straight draw, but giving me a pair of nines which at head-to-head might well be significant toward winning high.

Again I checked to him and he bet the fifty. I called. The ten of clubs hit the river giving me a straight. But a queen-jack or jack-eight would make a higher straight than mine. And there were many hands which would tie me. But, at this point, I was happy that there was no low since he probably had a better low draw than mine. Would you come out betting with my cards?

I have noted this situation many times and firmly believe that you have much more going with a "trap" check call. If he happens to have you beat, although unlikely, you save the raise since you would have to call. If you bet, looking at that board, he would probably fold if he did not have a straight. Perhaps, the biggest payoff in checking is that you might draw him in for yet another bet which you would simply call—and probably win.

Oh yes. I checked. He bet his nothing. I called and won.

## BLIND FISHING
Late one Friday night, I took a seat in a $5/$10 Omaha high-low game. As I folded the first two hands before the flop, I was happy to note that six and seven players called to see the flop. On the next hand, I saw the flop with an A 2 hand, but I ended up getting quartered (winning just one-fourth of the pot) and making a very small profit.

After surrendering several more hands before the flop, on my big blind, I picked up 10♠ 9♠ 5♥ 4♥. A player two spots to my left, who had raised before the flop twice in the last six hands, raised before the flop again. He got four callers including the little blind, and play came around to me. With two prime low cards (albeit the worst two) and being double-suited, I ventured a call, although this type of hand is marginal at best.

Any two 5-or-lower low cards flop a wheel only about one time in three hundred, but they do flop two of the other three wheel cards about one time in nine and then complete the wheel about 17% of those times. All in all, counting backdoor hits, any two prime low cards make a wheel with the five board cards about 3% of the time.

The flop was K♠ 6♠ 2♥. Intending to fold any bet, I checked. The player on my left bet, all four other players called around to me. For some unclear reason, I decided to "take one off." The turn card was the amazing A♠, which gave me both the third-nut flush and third-nut low.

I checked to see how many other players liked this card. It was checked all the way around to my right-hand (last) opponent, who bet. Although I fully expected him to have me beat one-way, I made what I consider an obvious raise (see the "Promo Raises" section in Chapter 4) to pressure the remaining opponents. This raise was certainly speculative, since with four checked opponents in back of me, there was a great risk that someone was trapping. Fortunately, three of these opponents folded. One opponent commented, "That tight ass always has the nuts." Only a calling station called; he was in almost every pot. The bettor on my right did not raise.

The fifth card was an ugly 4, which counterfeited my already dubious low. I checked and it went check all around. My 10-high flush beat my right-hand opponent's lesser flush, and my low, which had been best after the turn, now split low with the calling station's A 5. Thus, my fishy hand ended up with three-quarters of the pot.

Two rounds later, again on my big blind, the fates displayed their sense of humor by dealing me 10 8 5 4 double-suited in the same suits as in the above hand! The same player raised before the flop and got the same callers! Deja vu?

This time the flop came J 3 2 unsuited. I checked and the before-the-flop raiser bet. I called into the four-way action. The turn card was the 6♥, which gave me the current nut high and a gut straight flush draw.

Knowing well the fragility of my low straight, I bet out and hoped the leading bettor, the before-the-flop raiser, would raise and get a fold or two. He raised, but no one folded. Although almost half of the remaining cards would preserve my nut high, I figured someone else might have had a 5 4, so I just called.

Suppose the last card had been the 10♥ which would have improved my nut straight to a very low flush. I would have checked. It would have gone a bet, a raise, and a call. I probably would have folded my two-way loser and saved a few bucks as a nut-flush and an A 4 would have seemed destined to split up the pot.

Well, no. I was just supposing since that is what often happens! Actually, the last card was the 10♠. I still had high locked, but I might be tied. I checked in first seat, and the lead bettor bet as expected. Both players called. Now I felt I could raise. Even if I tied I wouldn't lose much.

The aggressive lead bettor reraised, and both callers finally gave it up and folded. I just called and expected to split the pot with an A 4. I did split the pot, but with another 5 4. He held a 2 3 4 5! Truly, in Omaha high-low, beauty is in the eyes of the beholder. Note that my raise did not gain any money, unless one of the folders held an A 5, the second-nut low.

Although these two nearly identical blind hands each showed a profit, I am not an advocate of playing the 5 4 holding as it has great second-best potential. But for blind-defending purposes, second and third nut holdings are often worth a small investment when things appear favorable. Looked at from a macro perspective, it's just another day at the office.

## BLIND THINKING

I once was playing in a delightfully loose $10/$20 Omaha high-low game in Costa Rica, where the average flop saw six-plus players. On my little blind of $5, I picked up J♣ 4♣ 6♦ 2♦. Five players called around to me. Clearly, investing five more dollars, one-fourteenth of the pot, would be correct with most hands, assuming you know enough to fold unless the flop is good for you. At those odds, any two prime low cards, here the 2 and 4, would be cost-effective. And having the 6 in addition made my call very sound.

It was seven-way action and the flop came A♦ 5♦ 6♥. This was a medium-good flop for me. Looking at it mathematically, the likelihood of none of the nine other players having been dealt a 2 3 was about 56% assuming that all 2 3 hands would be played in this loose game. That is the same percentage situation as an A 2 being held when you have an A 3. With six other players seeing the flop, the odds of no one else having a diamond flush draw are about one in four. And the pair of 6s gave me some additional high potential.

On second-nut low hands, I usually check to see who wants to bet. It's important to get the lay of the land, so to speak. If I have little or less high potential, and it goes bet and raise, I usually think it's right to fold a second-nut low before it gets expensive. I checked and the big blind checked. Then the next player bet. There were several folds and one call back to me. I called and so did the big blind.

It was now four-way action, and the turn card was the J♥, the second heart on board, giving me jacks and 6s. Although I might well have been beat in both directions (the lead bettor might have had a 2 3, and another player might have had aces-over), I believed it was very key to bet here to see if the flop-bettor would raise. If it went raise-reraise, I probably would have folded.

Note that I might actually have had the best hand in one direction, though not clear which way. But most important is that a raise by the flop-bettor at that point would actually have been *good*, since it might well have pressured both other players into folding. Then I would be a big favorite to win half the pot. At worst, at that point I had some chances of hitting a good last card, especially a 3, and possibly a dubious full-house or flush.

The big blind folded—fearing a raise?—but the flop-bettor just called, as did the other player. It was not clear where I stood at this juncture, except that it was good that the last caller didn't raise.

The last card was the 10♣. A king-queen now would have the nut high. I thought it would be silly for me to bet at this point, since I was fairly sure the next player would call—sometimes it is right to bet in three-handed situations when the second hand to act may be pressured (a hump bet)—and I certainly would not like being raised. But the other two players checked also.

I was rather surprised to scoop this pot. The flop-bettor had A K 4 3, third-nut low and aces. The other caller had a diamond draw and two low pair. Even though one or both might have called a bet after the last card, I still think it was correct for me to check.

# 4 AFTER THE FLOP

In Omaha, as in hold 'em, the flop is everything. There is perhaps no more exciting moment in all of poker when so much happens at one time. As these three cards flop upon the table, the best possible hands may go down the drain and some bad hands may turn into gold. But usually mathematics and justice prevail. Strategy lesson number one comes directly from the Kenny Rogers song: "You've got to know when to fold 'em." When it is not your flop, or worse, when it *is* someone else's flop, it is simply time to fold. So, fold 'em! Don't chase rainbows.

Omaha, however, especially four-card Omaha, has a very complex combinatorial probability aspect. In Texas hold 'em, usually you cannot afford to play for two card draws, when you need *both* the fourth and fifth cards to complete your hand. But, frequently in Omaha, in most normal betting structures where the bet after the flop is only half the maximum bet, the fact that you have several of these two-card draw possibilities adds enough equity to allow you to fish in with marginal holdings.

## PUSHING AND PULLING AT HIGH-LOW

In Omaha, and in poker in general, there are times when you **pull**, try to make it easy for opponents to put their money into the pot, and times when you **push**, try to push opponents out of the pot. You pull mainly when you have a super hand, with little chance of being outdrawn, or when you have a good draw and would like good odds on your investment. In early positions, you often *do not* raise before the flop with good hands because you do not want to discourage bad initial calls. That's also pulling. And if you hit a great flop, you usually continue to pull.

But most often, when the flop hits the table, you will not have a great hand. Much more frequently the flop contains something which you hope gives you an advantage or at least a slight edge over your opponents. It then is wise to change horses and push! Checking and calling with a slight edge is vastly inferior to grabbing the initiative, **driving**—especially for the first bet after the flop. If you do not bet, your opponent will not fold—and he might improve. So when you have a slight edge after the flop, most of the time you should try to push your opponents out with bets and raises thus making them forfeit their initial investments or pay more than their hands are worth. If the situation changes as it often does in Omaha, you might have to change your push-pull perspective several times over the course of a hand.

The following real-life hand served as a good example for two of my students. I was playing $5/$10 Omaha high-low split (8 or better for low) at Foxwoods in Connecticut and I picked up A♣ K♣ 4♥ 2♦. With four callers already in the pot, I raised before the flop, and two more players called cold in back of me. Seven-way action in a raised pot is good action even at Foxwoods, and even on a Saturday night!

It was quite clear to raise with four callers already in. In first seat you would merely call with this hand so as not to squelch the action since a raise makes it easier for the fish to correctly fold. But once there are several players trapped in front of you, it's fine if the players in back of you fold; you then get their later or last position. Having last position gives you a worthwhile edge in the subsequent play of all hands.

Note that an A 2 by itself is usually not a good raise unless accompanied by some other good cards. It flops a made low about 7% of the time and flops two low cards about 37% of the time, which low draw hits about 59% of the time. Overall, A 2-empty makes a low in five cards about 36% of the time, but about 7% are **backdoor**, made on the last two cards, and often folded before maturity. Also note that almost one-third of these lows are counterfeited by the presence of an ace or deuce on the board!

Thus, an A 2 empty is essentially a good draw, somewhat similar to a nut flush couple like ace-other. And again, with both of these holdings, you would rather pull players in than push them out.

A 2 3 or A 2 4 will produce winners almost twice as frequently as ace-empty, making lows about 49% of the time with only about one-eighth of these lows are counterfeited. If two different low cards hit the flop, which happens about 28% of the time, then a safe nut low is made about 72% of the time. These extra percentages justify raising before the flop in late seats and more aggressive playing in general, depending mostly on your high prospects and the current size of the pot.

With my A♣ K♣ 4♥ 2♦ hand, the flop came K♠ 3♠ 2♣. This may look like a good flop to some, but it is the most dangerous kind (medium-high and unsafe low) and can cost you big money on the last two rounds. You would rather have two clubs and two non-duplicating low cards as the deuce used up your counterfeit protection.

The caller directly in front of me bet. What should I do? With a really good flop, like those mentioned above, I should simply call here to pull and hope for good attendance in case one of my draws hit and it is cheaper if nothing hit. In this case, though, since there were a lot of chips in the pot, a raise is a clear choice to try to pressure the weaker highs to improve my kings and deuces for high chances. Here, pushing is a higher priority than keeping in the weaker non-nut draws.

The player in back of me reraised, one of the blinds also called, and I had no reason not to cap it. Then, with four-way action, the turn card was the great 8♣! My slight edge had turned into the temporary nut low, the best low unless the last card was an ace or 4, and a nut club draw for high. Time to pull.

Since it seemed unlikely to get checked out, I checked. The player in back of me made the $10 bet as expected, and both other players called. With the current nut low and some good high prospects—nut club draw, two pair and wheel draw—I raised according to plan. The play went call, then reraise (!), and then the holder of the fourth hand said, "Cap it!" All players called.

Again with four-way action, the last card was the J♠. It seemed likely that someone had hit a flush. There was a bet, a raise, and a call. I called, expecting to be quartered, likely to tie for nut low in view of previous action.

The bad news was that two other players also had the nut A 4, which meant a three-way split of low. The great news was that no one had spades or could beat my kings over! Although this kind of win is lucky, it's actually one of the reasons for raising *after* the flop. I ended up getting the rare two thirds of this healthy pot (one-half plus one-sixth).

When you play Omaha high-low, you have much less knowledge as to what specific opponents are likely to be holding than you have when you are playing straight high. Thus, you often play Omaha high-low on general principles.

I sometimes compare that to landing an airplane in a fog. Knowing whether you should generally push or pull often helps dictate your best strategy.

## SECOND BEST

Perhaps the most delicate and difficult hands to play in Omaha high-low are second-best one-way holdings after the flop. When you hold the nut hand or draw, at least you know that you belong in the pot, although it is not always clear whether you want to push or pull. But when you flop a second-best holding, it is sometimes best to get out cheap right after the flop. This is usually a difficult judgment to make, especially in early position since second-best holdings play best in late position. Often you do not find out that it was right to get out early until you've invested a bet or two.

The classic second-best low example is when your hand includes an A 3 and the flop hits with two or three low cards with different ranks from 4 through 8. The classic second-best high hand example is when your hand includes the king and another spade and the flop hits with two or three spades and no pair.

Most inexperienced Omaha high-low players automatically play the above two holdings whatever the cost. But most good players know that it is often right to fold these second best hands, especially when there are raises. These second best hands are often squeezed unmercifully after the fourth and last cards, when the betting limit doubles. Although they occasionally hit a miracle last card (in this example, a deuce) and win half a pot, much more often they suffer a big loss.

When the raising starts, wise players usually avoid fishing in with second-best holdings on the last two doubled rounds.

But often, after the flop, especially when there are no raises, it is correct to see one more card since you might draw the nuts, here, a deuce. Or perhaps no one has an A 2 on this hand. And in the absence of subsequent raises, you might call to the showdown.

What are the underlying odds of your second nuts hand being a winner or being tied? Assuming that no A 2 would fold before the flop, computer simulations tell us that there will be an A 2 holding in one or more of the other nine starting hands about half of the time. There will be another A 3 holding which ties you, so you're quartered, about 40% of the time. Because of those two possibilities, your A 3 will be the single best low only about 30% of the time. And even if you are the best low after the flop, your A 3 will be counterfeited, some call it **bricked,** on one of the last two cards about one-quarter of the time. And low never gets more than half of the pot.

The only good news is that if you are being chased by only one other low contender, often only one of your counterfeit cards will actually make you lose. For example, if you are being chased by a 2 3 and a 3 hits, your live ace still beats the chaser's live deuce. The possibility of your A 3 losing by being counterfeited is somewhat offset by hands where you win by counterfeiting, that is, where you were beat after the flop by an A 2 holding, but then one of the remaining three deuces hits the board thus counterfeiting the A 2 hand and giving you the nut low.

Normally, when you flop a second-best made hand in early seat, you check or call and hope for inaction. Some players advocate betting or raising to check for raisers, a find-out-where-I'm-at-play, while the betting is cheap. But perhaps the main problem with two-way games is that you can never be sure who is going in which direction or who is making tactical raises. All you know for sure is that it is going to cost you money to find out.

When the flop has only two low cards or two flush cards and you have a draw instead of an already made hand, raises are much less likely. But although you may get to see the fourth card cheaply, unless you turn your nut card, you usually cannot afford to play a second best hand when faced with raises after fourth street if you are in contention for only half the pot.

If you have at least marginal holdings or better in both directions, everything changes! With that sort of hand, you usually raise after the flop to shake out other marginal one-way hands. (See the section on "Promo Raises" in Chapter 3).

If you hold a king-other of a suit and three of that suit hit the flop, what are the odds that the ace-other are out against you in a ten-handed game? If you are playing in a loose rule game or perhaps in a *heavenly game*, you will see the flop with most four-card starting hands containing an ace-other. The term **heavenly game** was coined recently when a player asked me, "If an average of more than five players seeing the flop is called a 'rule game' (Cappelletti's Rule), what do you call it when seven or more players are seeing the flop on every hand?" I replied, "I call it heaven." Surprisingly, there are many heavenly games around, although mostly at low stakes.

Thus, if, in a ten-handed game, most hands containing an ace-other see the flop, then computer simulations tell us that the ace-other holding will be out against you about one-third of the time. If your flush is made on the flop, that is three spades come on the flop, and there are several raises after the flop, you are probably in trouble. Unless you have other good prospects, you should probably fold immediately, especially if a low is present.

Even if the higher flush is not present, the board might pair and you might lose anyway. When there is no low, one or zero low cards in flop, it is unlikely that there will be more than one raise after a flush flop. At limit Omaha high-low, you should occasionally pay off someone who might well be bluffing on a high-only pot.

Note also that whenever two or three different low cards come on the flop, a low flop, calling even with the nut high draw is a marginal undertaking because of the likelihood of a split pot. Thus, calling with a hand that might be drawing dead is even more dubious.

The bottom line in all of this is that when you're playing Omaha high-low, you can save money by not chasing with second-best holdings unless the signs are very favorable.

## COMBINATION HANDS IN OMAHA HIGH-LOW

The same concepts for combination hands in straight high Omaha can be extended to high-low Omaha. And playing these combination hands correctly after the flop is one of the most skill-demanding aspects of high-low Omaha.

In four-card high Omaha, it is usually correct after the flop to play only hands containing one or more primary holdings. A **primary holding** consists of two of your four cards which work with the three-card flop to constitute a poker hand of sufficient merit that, by itself or with just one additional card, rates to win frequently enough to justify playing further. A **combination hand** is a hand which does not have any primary holdings but does contain several lesser holdings which individually would not be good enough to play, but in combination, add up to playable odds, especially when there is a large starting pot because of raises before the flop.

When, after the flop, you have one or more inferior four-card holdings, and perhaps several three-card secondary holdings—which could improve to primary holdings with the right turn card, the total of all these lesser holdings may well justify seeing the fourth board card, especially if you're in a late seat or when raises are unlikely. If there's no improvement, many combination hands should fold after the fourth card.

The junk variation of a combination hand includes one or more lesser junk four-card holdings such as two low pairs, low four flushes, and/or low straight draws, and ample secondary holdings. It is difficult to estimate a general win rate for the junk variations, but they do well when played aggressively against passive opponents. Playing these hands is very dangerous, delicate, and game dependent. Position, presence, knowledge of the tendencies of the other players, and generally very good judgment are all required to play these successfully. Note that these junk combination hands are less likely to be played profitably in very aggressive games.

In high-low Omaha, how often do you raise with an A 2 holding only to catch two high cards in the flop? Often? Don't worry, all is not lost. A secondary low draw, preferably based on the two lock cards—that is, A 2, A 3, or 2 3, can be a valuable addition to various high combinations. Note that these two-card low draws win about 16% of the time. Although low wins are usually only half the pot, these additional winning prospects often tilt the percentages in favor of seeing one more card, especially if you can see it cheaply.

Suppose you raise before the flop with A♠ 10♠ 4♥ 2♦ and flop the usual K♠ J♥ 4♣. Your best asset here is the inside straight draw to a queen, but you also have several two-card secondary draws. The approximate win rates in the following chart were obtained by running this hand on Mike Caro's Poker Probe against five random opponents.

|  | Makes | Approx. Wins |
|---|---|---|
| Straights (Q or 5 3) | 17.8% | 12% |
| Flush | 4.2% | 3.6% |
| Full House | 2.7% | 1.8% |
| Other highs | 50% | 5% |
| Low | 16% | 14% |

Note that the above high wins are full pot wins, whereas the low wins are merely half pot wins. All win figures are adjusted to include ties. Probably the best estimates of overall win rate with this sort of hand are somewhere between one-quarter and one-third of the time, depending mostly on the number of players. Thus, if the pot is large (you raised, remember?), you would certainly like to see one more card, especially if the price is right. When I played the above hand, the next card was the Q♠! It not only scooped the pot for me, but also gave me a shot at the royal jackpot, worth $500 at the casino I was playing at.

## POST-FLOP RAISING

I was playing $10/$20 Omaha high-low at Foxwoods, when a lady with a charming Southern accent commented that she had never seen anyone raise as often after the flop as I did. It was one of those sessions where it had seemed right to raise almost every time it was my turn.

Although the after-the-flop raise is probably your most powerful and effective weapon in Omaha high-low, it is equally important to know when not to raise. To put this another way, although in Omaha high-low you often like to push after the flop, sometimes it is preferable to pull.

For example, in Omaha high-low, when you are drawing to a nut low, nut flush or other big draw after the flop, normally it would be silly to raise. Not only would you rather invest less in case you do not hit it, but, even more importantly, you do not want to make it difficult to call. More players in the pot means a higher ratio of return if you do hit it, and a greater likelihood of getting paid off. You might want to raise, however, when you have both a nut draw and a marginal holding in the other direction.

Generally, it is most important and most effective and sometimes even critical to raise when you have two-way marginal holdings. If you can substantially narrow the field, you dramatically increase your chances of backing into high or low. Other reasons for aggressive raising are to get your opponents accustomed to calling your frequent big bets for when you have good hands, and to gather more information, especially when certain tight opponents call cold.

Test your after-the-flop judgment in the following loose Omaha situations:

1. You hold A♠ Q♠ 10♣ 4♦ and the flop comes:
   A) J♠ 10♠ 7♥ or
   B) J♣ 10♥ 7♦

With four or more players seeing the flop, the player on your right lead bets. Do you fold, call, or raise?

With the nut flush draw, flop A, you have little reason to raise. But without the big flush draw, flop B, if you are going to call, then you should raise and try to move as much competition as possible.

2. You hold A♣ K♣ J♥ 3♦ and the flop comes:
   A) K♦ 10♠ 2♥ or
   B) K♦ 10♠ 7♥

With four or more players, someone bets in front of you. Do you fold, call, or raise?

With the first flop, although there are some high-oriented reasons to raise, I would most often simply call, especially against fish that might fold a raise (since I hold the best three-card low). There is much to be said for keeping your investment low until you see the next card (you welcome 4s through 8s in addition to your high card hits). Note that with the second flop, a strong additional reason for raising after the flop is to insure that an A 2 holding cannot call cheaply (you will hit a backdoor low about one time in six).

3. You hold A♠ J♠ 8♥ 3♦ and the flop comes 10♥ 8♦ 7♣. With four players, the player in front of you bets. Should you fold, call, or raise?

Although I normally fold second-low draws in multi-way pots, unless I have high potential, if the lead bettor in front of you tends to bet aggressively on skimpy values and there are players in back of you who know how to fold, you might try an exciting raise! It would be unsound merely to call with this hand in a multi-way pot.

If your raise results in your playing head-to-head with the lead bettor, you have reasonable prospects, and your opponent will probably check to you after fourth street. If one of the two later players cold-calls your raise, he probably has an A 2 or a good high holding. Unless you turn a good card, you might decide to leave the arena next round. If you merely call, you would not get useful information when one or both of the other players call. Thus, raising not only might narrow the field, but it also might get you better information to guide your judgment next round.

## FLOP COMING: HIGH FLOPS

There are many situations in poker where it is correct to bet on a hand which must draw favorably in order to have value. Sometimes, a come or draw may have enough potential value to justify a bet. For example, when playing Omaha, sometimes you have so many outs, outstanding draw cards which will make your hand, that you actually are a favorite to win half the pot or more. And sometimes percentages suggest trying a bluff bet when you have one or more comes which might bail you out if you are called.

When playing loose Omaha high low it is frequently correct to bet after the flop on a come or even on mere potential. And perhaps the most important reason to make that bet is to prevent opponents from gaining a free card which might cost you a half or even a whole pot. A second reason to bet after the flop on mere potential is that occasionally either everyone folds, although this is rare in a loose game, or you get only one straggling caller who often folds on the next round or who you might end up beating.

In this section, we will discuss betting high flop situations. Suppose you are playing Omaha high low in first position with a wonderful high hand, ace and jack of spades and jack and ten of hearts. In first seat you called because you normally do not raise in loose Omaha high low with a high only hand, and because there is six-way action. The flop comes king-nine-five rainbow, which essentially misses you except for the inside-straight draw. The blinds both check to you. What would you do?

Playing loose Omaha high low, I consider it clear to bet here because with two high cards in the flop, it is imperative to make the low hands either fold or pay more than a backdoor low draw is worth. Even though anyone holding a king, at this point, has a better hand than yours, and even though you might get raised, nevertheless, you will win more money in the long run by betting now.

Perhaps the only exception to betting a marginal high hand at this point would be if there was an extremely active player sitting to your left who you are quite sure will bet if you check. Even in that situation it is probably right for you to bet since your bets are more likely to get opponents to fold than his and also he might raise—and you certainly do not mind being raised by someone who often has very little.

But keep in mind that the main consideration here is that if the hand was checked around, that would be a strategic disaster for you! When you play a high only hand, letting the low hands back in by allowing them to see a free low card on the fourth card (the "turn") might easily end up costing you half a pot or more. You could easily lose high (especially a "back in" type high) to a hand that would have folded a bet after the flop.

Otherwise put, from your perspective, someone must bet—and if someone has to bet, it might as well be you! By betting, you figuratively slam down your gauntlet and proclaim to the world that you intend to contest this pot! And most often, the total of good things that can happen by betting easily outweigh the cost of the bet. As the driver, there is always some chance that you will win now or later by default. Even if you do get raised, which should certainly narrow the action even further, at least you now have more information about what would be best to do after the last two bets.

Are there some general exceptions to the strategy of betting a high flop with almost any high hand? Very few – the one obvious exception is when you flop a super hand (the nuts and very unlikely to be outdrawn). With all pulling hands, you want more opponents in the pot, as opposed to the usual pushing hand where you want competition out.

Note that after a very strong flop, such as a high pair or a high flop with three cards of the same suit, you might check on the theory that whoever has the big fit with the board should do the betting, although this is more likely to get folded around than betting a normal or jagged flop. Also note that if someone does bet this flop, you will clearly fold, unless the bettor frequently bets on nothing. You do not want to call down and pay off a player who is unknown or who usually has cards. Thus there is some chance that you are now folding to a player who is taking advantage of an opportunity you missed.

If you had opted to bet the strong flop—a speculation with your medium high hand—and then someone raised, then you are less likely to be folding to an opportunist, especially if you have a tight image. The one unit you invest might easily win the pot if no one has a good hand or might prevent someone from seeing a nice fourth card.

So my advice is, after a high flop, if you have enough to seriously consider calling, then you probably have enough to bet, unless you have a pulling hand where you want opponents in. Next we will discuss "flop coming" with low flops.

## FLOP COMING: LOW FLOPS
When playing loose Omaha high low it is frequently correct to bet after the flop on a come or even on mere potential. And perhaps the most important reason to make that bet is too prevent opponents from getting a free card which might cost you a half or even a whole pot. We've already discussed making these aggressive bets after a high flop.

What are your inclinations about betting a nut low draw at Omaha high low? For example, suppose your four cards are an ace-deuce and two high cards, and a four-six-king hit the flop. Do you lead bet? A lot of players like to wait until they actually make the nut low before they voluntarily put more money into the pot. We all know how often these two-card nut low draws don't get there (miss over 40%). And pessimists often check even after making the nut low in fear of being quartered.

We have all heard advice that "you should only bet a nut low draw when you also have a third low (backup) card in your hand" because three low cards hit a low over 70%. I do not agree with that advice.

My advice is that under most conditions you should bet any nut low draw after the flop, especially if you think it might get checked around (that would be a strategic disaster from your point of view). You should bet not just because you have good chances of winning half the pot, but because *you belong* in the pot and perhaps some of your opponents do not! Think of it as the price of admission. Do *not* give free cards to those who might beat you if they get a free card! If you have a nut low draw, probably the only good reason not to bet the flop is that the pot is relatively small and you think your checking might induce the other players to bet.

In order to see the whole picture, let's look at hands that we call pulling hands. Sometimes, you do *not* bet or raise because you want more opponents in the pot. Suppose you flop four jacks and the other flop card is a high card. Since you do not have to worry about splitting the pot (low can not make), and you can safely assume that you will win the pot, then you might check after the first two rounds so that no one will fold. Perhaps someone else will bet or perhaps some will improve enough to bet or call your bet on the final round. The main point is you do not want to pressure anyone into folding. You want to pull in as much competition as possible. You would only bet or raise if it seemed likely that no one would fold

Similarly, when you are drawing for a nut flush in a high-only pot, when the board is unlikely to make a low, sometimes you want to pull in competition. And checking tends to lessen your investment—and everyone else's. However, you sometimes prefer to push if you have other promotable high or low values. The main point here is that if you hit your nut flush, you would like as many opponents in the pot as possible. More opponents make a bigger pot and make it more likely that you will be paid off after you hit. So a nut high draw absent other high or low prospects is also a pulling situation.

When you are drawing to a nut low, how do you distinguish between pushing aggressively bet or raise and pulling situations? You must use your judgment to decide whether or not you want to pull more opponents into the pot to pay you off if you hit low or whether to push and try to narrow the field to improve your chances of backing into high. When two nut low hands raise each other furiously after the flop and/or turn and push out all or most of the competition, it is not unusual for high to be won with a mere pair.

Note that when it is close between pushing and pulling, you should probably push. It would be bad economics to pull in an extra caller to pay off your nut low, if that caller narrowly beats you out of high. Essentially you have to evaluate your own high potential, then try to judge who might have a high draw as opposed to trips or two pair—a **made** hand—by the way they are betting and by the way they normally play. Of course, putting players on hands is tricky business at Omaha high low—but aggressive play based on informed guesses does pay off in the long run.

Does this same philosophy apply to raising with a nut low draw after the flop? Answer, yes, but to a lesser extent. Again it depends mostly on your high potential versus your low values. The concept is best explained by an example.

Suppose you hold a 2-3-4-Q in six-way action (unraised). The flop comes ace-seven-queen off suit. You are likely to make the nut low over 70% of the time. The player in front of you bets. I would raise here mostly to promote the high potential of my queens. If the queen in the flop had been a jack, I would just call because I would have nothing for high. Or if the seven in the flop had been a five, thereby giving me three cards to make a wheel, I would just call to pull in more opponents.

But all of the above is certainly subject to your feel of the table. Quite often, especially in close situations, you bet or raise because it feels right based on the momentum of what's been happening on previous hands. Omaha high low in many respects is more of an art form than a science.

## AFTER THE FLOP PROMO RAISES

If you've forgotten what I mean by a promo raise, take another look at the section called *Promo Raises Before the Flop* in Chapter 3. The term **promotional raise** ("promo raise" or just "promo") originally was used in reference to certain Omaha high-low after-the-flop situations. Promoting lesser cards into winners is indeed one of the main skill areas in Omaha high-low. Anyone can win with the nuts. Making opportunistic investments to promote losers into winners requires both brains and brass.

Let's say you're playing Omaha high-low (8 or better), and you pick up A♣ J♣ 7♠ 4♠. With this hand, you call a six-player raised pot in big blind position. The flop comes Q♠ 8♠ 6♥. That's two spades working with your 7 and 4. Hence, you have a low flush draw, a fourth best low draw that needs two cards to be the nuts, and a non-nut inside straight draw. The little blind lead bets in front of you. Do you fold, call, or raise?

Calling is bad. If you call, whatever you draw rates to get beat either by the nuts or by a slightly better hand, a second rate hand that often would have folded a raise. Only fish call with draws that rate to lose if they hit. If the game is very loose and the opponents to your left have very little fear of raises, then you should fold.

Against normal human competition—those who live in fear of Omaha like the rest of us—your best play is to raise, because of the already large starting pot. If half the players fold, you will usually be in reasonable position. With this flop, the only good calls of your raise are an A 2, trips, the nut flush draw, or a big wraparound straight draw, unlikely cards. The lead bettor might well have one of those good holdings, but it is unlikely that more than one other exists in the four hands yet to act.

Your promotional raise will often cause half of the players to fold! You might well fold second-class holdings such as a 2 3 or even an A 3, and you might also fold a higher flush draw or a 9 7 which beats your straight if a 5 turns. Note that you do have inferior holdings and will have to back down if there is heat. Your current investment is entirely speculative, and you must concede it if there is too much competition later. Even if the fourth card is a 5 or the 2 or 3 of spades, you are deathly afraid of raises, though on a good day, you might scoop.

Thus your game plan is to invest in the two-way promotional raise, hope to seriously narrow attendance (thus promoting your third-rate holdings), and then catch enough to call—if there are no raise wars later. Against only one or two other players, there are many ways you could win half the pot. And if the lead bettor does not hit, you could end up with the whole pot.

In high-low Omaha, it is usually a good investment to raise after the flop when you have two-way prospects which include a third-rate prospect that might win if a second-rate prospect can be folded. As in hold 'em, it is often sound to be very aggressive at Omaha high-low after the flop. If all of your prospects are third rate holdings, it takes good after-flop judgment to determine whether a promo raise is a good investment.

It is true that the two-way promo raise, as someone once said, is like "playing both ends against the middle." And it is also true that sometimes you end up with the middle—that is, nothing! However, the gods of Omaha high-low do seem to have a sense of humor, and it is almost absurd how often bold moves and unforeseen cards present you with both ends!

## THE DOUBLE PROMO RAISE AT HIGH-LOW

As I stated in the preceding section, one of the most useful weapons at Omaha high-low is the promo raise after the flop, where you hope to pressure marginal second-class holdings into folding, thereby promoting your third-class holdings which then might win half the pot. Some examples of good third-class holdings that are good enough to beat other inferior holdings which might be promoted by a promo raise are a 2 3 for low or a queen-other suited flush draw, where an A 3 low draw or king-high flush draw might fold an after-the-flop raise since a non-nut draw normally should not be played in the face of big betting.

A prudent Omaha player makes a promo raise only when he also has a sound competitive holding in the other direction. Raising with a third-rate holding in one direction is actually sound if you have an adequate holding in the other direction to partially justify the investment. Although very aggressive Omaha high-low players might make instinctive promo raises even without a sound holding in the other direction—and, indeed, their raises will occasionally work—those of us that like money are reluctant to risk a bigger investment than a hand is worth. You must realize that Omaha high-low is truly a fast and loose game—if you play loose, your money goes fast.

What if, instead of a sound competitive holding in the other direction, you hold yet another marginal or third-rate holding, which you also might promote via the same promo raise? Can two marginal holdings add up to soundness? Quite often at Omaha high-low, if the starting pot is large enough because of before-the-flop raises, many risky actions which would normally be financially unwise actually have a positive expectation or at least become marginal.

It is my opinion that these double promo raises are often sound, but it does depend on the game and the tenacity of your opponents. When the starting pot becomes large, promo raises are less likely to make the second-rate competition fold. Thus, a lot of opponent-reaction judgment is involved in making promo raises.

Say you're playing $5/$10 Omaha high-low. You call in late seat with a Q♣ 4♣ 3♠ 2♥. There is six-way action. The flop comes J♥ 7♣ 5♣, giving you a queen-high flush draw and the third-nut low draw (that is, if an 8, 6, or 4 hits, then both A 2 and A 3 beat you for low). Both blinds check, and there is a bet, a fold, and a call in front of you.

Both of your draws are third rate and dangerous! Since you have no nut draw, should you make the conservative fold? Calling is probably a losing action. But a raise might work! If you raise, quite often any second rate hands in back of you might fold. What are your approximate odds of winning half or all of the pot against two or three opponents?

In a loose game with ten or eleven players, it is slightly better than 50% likely that there is an A 2 present. Consider it even more likely with six players in a tight game. If one of the three opponents in back of you has only an A 3, he should probably fold rather than call your raise, which might get reraised. Similarly, an opponent with the king-high flush draw should fold your raise. It is quite possible that both blinds in back of you will fold, which not only increases your chances of winning, but might well get the hand checked around to you on the next round of betting. This would allow you to check and see the last card for free. Who knows—maybe the suited ace will hit the table!

Although these double promo raises after-the-flop are rare, more frequently the concept of "raise instead of call" applies to hands with marginal holdings in both directions where your poker judgment tells you to blast away. No guarantees on all this!

# 5 THE LAST TWO ROUNDS

The last two rounds of betting in Omaha high-low—that is, the rounds on the turn and the river—are generally like the last two rounds in any poker game. The seeds have already been sown, and now comes harvest time. Hopefully you are the "harvestor" rather than the "harvestee."

Both of these rounds are at the maximum bet, which is usually double the initial bet. Note that if just one bet with no raise occurs each round, you put in two-thirds of your total contribution to the pot on these last two rounds. In other words, all of the high level strategy that we have been discussing about what you bet before the flop and immediately after the flop accounts for merely one-third of your entire investment in an unraised pot. These last two rounds are the big bet rounds. This is the key time to know when to hold 'em and know when to fold 'em. One of the cardinal principles of Omaha high-low, as in other flop games, is not to fish in for these big bets with inadequate cards.

On the other hand, this is one of the better times to make hay if the sun is shining on your winning hand. Although most really big pots begin with before- and after-flop raises, many dollars are won starting with this maximum-bet fourth round. In essence, what poker is all about is being able to bet and get more money in the pot when you have the winning hand and to fold or minimize your losses when you happen to have a loser. At this fourth card juncture, Omaha is basically like any other poker game. There are, however, some very interesting strategic fourth round considerations—particularly in dubious situations when it is not clear whose pot it is.

## LITTLE POTS

First let us examine the **unwanted pot** situation—when the bet was checked around after the flop. At this point, the pot itself is hardly worth fighting over, unless there were some before-the-flop raises. In theory, since you have very little to protect, there is little reason to take risks. There is always the possibility of running into a timid soul or trapper who actually has a hand.

But we all know that if you can successfully steal a few of these little ante pots, they'll add up to a worthwhile amount. And your sporting and competitive poker instincts might occasionally move you to go for the steal or to try to pick off somebody else's bluff. So when should you invest a double bet? The answer is that a lot depends on your overall game-plan choreography and image.

In Omaha, it is not simply a matter of how much money you might win or lose in these little pot situations. An equal, or even a more important consideration is your image that day. These little pots are a prime opportunity for "image investing"—that is, you are investing money not only in winning more money, but also in developing and enhancing your image.

When you make a double bet with a speculative hand, a hand with less than full values, in the eyes of the world, you are bluffing. Since it is good to be "loved" at Omaha, it is good PR occasionally to get caught with your hand in the cookie jar. It is difficult to quantify just how much it might be worth, but this sort of PR is definitely worth something. You might easily receive two or three additional callers on your next few winning hands. Thus, there are two equally important reasons to bet. Good, loose-aggressive Omaha players not only show a plus in these situations by winning, but also gain "love points" when they get caught.

One of the main reasons why you play quite tight for a little pot on fourth street is that everyone has had a free chance to improve, and the higher the card, the more likely someone has improved. If that person is you, and you now probably have a winner, by all means bet—and hope that one or more fish will think that you are trying some of the above-mentioned stealing nonsense. But if you did not improve substantially, why not let some other genius try to the steal this nothing pot? Save your money and bluffing license for more significant endeavors.

Although general poker principles tell you to take an occasional sporting shot to steal one of these up-for-grabs little pots, for strategic reasons, you might prefer to sit back, let your honesty shine through, and let the other aggressive players contest this small pot—especially if you tend to drive bluff, which is mostly done on high-only hands, fairly frequently. It would be very unfortunate if some random player decided to call you on a big driving bluff just because he remembered your "dishonesty" when you tried to bluff on one of these small pots.

When you try to catch someone bluffing by calling a double bet, there is also an image consideration involved. When you expose your less-than-adequate calling hand, whether you win or lose, it is usually good PR to tell the world that you call everything and anything. An observer might choose not to try to bluff you on a subsequent hand.

Note that if you are not playing Omaha with a loose-aggressive image, there is much less reason to stray into what is possibly someone else's pot. Someone might well be sitting back with a good hand and a big net. Do not reward players who do not bet their cards adequately by betting their cards for them. Again the key strategic principle in little pot participation is this one: be acutely aware of the PR impact as well as the monetary profit involved.

## DRIVING AFTER THE LAST TWO ROUNDS

Let us now look at one of the most important strategic considerations in all of poker—whether to continue driving. You liked the flop at least enough to bet. You had several callers but no raisers. Had there been so much as one raise, it would be an entirely different ballgame.

If you hit a potentially winning card on fourth street, you should continue driving about two-thirds of the time, unless the game is loose enough that trapping almost always works. The remaining third of the time can be used for trapping, varying your style, and protecting your future aborted drives. It is at least twice as likely that someone will bet when you're playing high-low as it is when you're playing straight high! Thus check-raising is even more successful at Omaha high-low as at straight high.

If the bet gets checked around on fourth street, it is not nearly as potentially disastrous as it would be just after the flop. Most of the players who fold on fourth street are not going to win the pot anyway (note that strategic difference from the all important after-the-flop betting). Given that you just hit a good card, rarely will you lose the pot by missing this bet. There are some good arguments for almost always checking when you hit a super fourth card.

At straight high Omaha, the last two rounds of betting, usually at the double size limit, present many opportunities for the expert to exercise his skill and judgment in reading the opponents and then perhaps in making good percentage moves. At Omaha high-low, it is much more difficult to read the opponents correctly. Even the best players must proceed more on general principles than on deep brilliant moves. However, general principles sometimes can be applied with considerable skill and psychology.

Just as all good Omaha high-low players know that they must avoid getting squeezed by the brutal and terribly expensive raising that sometimes occurs on the last two rounds, unless they have a lock in one direction. All good Omaha players also know that these rounds are indeed one of the best times to make money. Although a player with a lock-low hand is often reluctant to cap out the betting because he fears getting quartered, sometimes the lock-low will risk a raise or two, especially with some high potential. But many Omaha experts tend not to over squeeze a poor fish caught in the middle. It turns off the fish and sometimes resembles collusion—even if the good players do not know each other. Plus, there is always the possibility of getting quartered.

If the flop contains two or more high cards, then the game essentially reverts to straight high Omaha. If the flop contains exactly one low card, then at least one of the high hands should bet to get the lows out and to maximize the chances of winning the whole pot.

Note that drive bluffs after a high flop are the most successful bluffs in Omaha high-low. During a normal good session, for every ten pots of which you win half or more, perhaps one or two come from drive bluffs—even if you have lost several drive bluff attempts. Thus, on many occasions, the one or two drive-bluff pots that you grab will be the margin between winning and losing.

If you aggressively bet high flops too frequently, however, one or more players might notice and take counter measures which would seriously reduce your effectiveness. Thus, to a large extent, your high-flop bluffing frequency should be determined by the usual calling frequency of the remaining callers. After a while, you may develop valuable instincts so that you often know in advance whether the chasers are going to call you.

If there are two or more low cards in the flop, the high hand rates to share the pot about three-quarters of the time. Welcome to the world of high-low. High-low is a whole different ballgame than straight high, and new strategies apply. Since the high hand rates to get only half of the pot, all of the expectations applicable to straight high Omaha are out the window—unless you have some compensating low equities also.

Of course, what you and everyone else really want is a "no brainer," a winning hand—high, low or both—that you really do not have to think about much. In high-low situations, you simply bet it every time it is your turn. Because of the bi-directionality, both highs and lows might be betting. Thus, it is roughly twice as likely that someone will bet. And it might as well be you, since betting says little about your hand. In straight high Omaha, betting gives away more information about your hand than checking does. But in high-low, checking says more, in a negative manner, about your hand than betting.

So if you want to build the pot, the percentage action is simply to bet and hope for a raise, which you might reraise—that gets three bets into the pot. Raises are fairly likely. You only check with a good hand when you strongly suspect that someone else will probably bet but probably will not raise. Note that the check-raise gets two bets into the pot and you seldom want to risk having it checked around.

Just after the flop, you may want to jack up the stakes on marginal or partially made hands, two high pairs, for example, especially if you're in last or near last position. You're operating on the theory that if you do not bet, there will be a nothing pot, and betting should narrow the field. Even in last position, though, it is anti-percentage to drive high come hands, unless you have other equities. It is sound to drive low come hands to promote marginal highs. Note that even if you manage to push out all of the official · high competition, if you have poor high holdings, one of the other low hands will beat you for high.

Generally, in high-low flop situations, you drive mainly with good two-way hands, with nut or near-nut high hands, with good low hands which also have marginal high holdings, and sometimes with two-way marginal holdings.

## BIG DRAWS

Like straight high Omaha, Omaha high-low is often thought of as a last card roulette. The player with the "most numbers covered," so to speak, is most likely to win. Unlike in hold 'em or in most other forms of poker, in Omaha, the player doing the betting before the last card, even if he's holding the current nuts, often has fewer winning last cards than players holding one or more big draws.

In Omaha high-low, a player drawing to a nut low who's holding the two lowest low cards—for example, a player holding A 2 in hand with a 7 8 on the table—would make his nut low with any of sixteen cards, in this case, any 3, 4, 5, or 6. If he held the three lowest cards (for example, A 2 3), he would make a nut low with twenty-one cards (four 4s, 5s or 6s, and three aces, 2s or 3s).

The biggest high draws are straight draws. Flush draws normally have nine outstanding cards which complete the hand: namely the thirteen cards of the suit minus the two on board and the two in your hand. A pocket pair matching one of the board cards ("a set" or "trips") has ten outs to make a full house or four-of-a-kind (one quad card plus three of each of the other board cards). But the biggest straight draws in Omaha can have as many as twenty outs!

For those of you who have not seen these catalogued before, the following list of 20-card draws should improve your understanding of all big straight draws:

| Type | Your hand | Board | Chances of Making |
|------|-----------|-------|-------------------|
| Eye | 9 8 6 5 | 10 7 4 | 30% (non-nuts) |
| Double-eye | 9 8 5 4 | 7 6 | 30% (non-nuts) |
| Two hole | 9 8 6 4 | 10 7 5 | 30% (non-nuts) |
| Two hole | 9 7 5 4 | 8 6 3 | 30% (non-nuts) |
| High triple | J 8 7 6 | 10 9 5 4 | 50% (non-nuts) |
| Low triple | 8 7 6 3 | 10 9 5 4 | 50% (non-nuts) |
| Quadruple | 8 7 6 5 | 10 9 4 3 | 50% (non-nuts) |

Note that all 20-card draws make a straight when one of the four hand cards (4x3=12) or one of the two end cards (2x4=8) is dealt to the board (hence the total: 12+8=20). A 20-card draw makes a straight about 45% of the time on the last card and about 70% of the time with two cards to go.

Test your knowledge on this one: Say you're playing no-limit Omaha with a hand of 9 8 6 5 and you flop 10 7 4 offsuit. You go all-in and get called by A 10 10 7. Who is the favorite? (Answer at the end of this chapter).

An example of the classic 17-card draw is the hand 9 7 5 with a board of 8 6. All other 17-card draws are similar to the 20-card draws given above, but with one hand card fewer. For example, you could hold 9 8 6 and catch a board of 10 7 5, or you could hold 9 8 5 with a board of 7 6. A 17-card draw makes a straight about 38% of the time on the last card and about 62% of the time with two cards to go. Note that the other hand and board cards may change these percentages slightly.

There are generally three problems with most big straight draws. First, when the board has two cards of the same suit, the value of your straight draw decreases about 20% because of flush possibilities. Second, although hitting your straight on the last card precludes pairing the board, if you make your straight on fourth street the value of your hand decreases by about 20% because of full house possibilities. Third, when you make the straight with one of the higher cards (either of your top two hand cards), it is usually a non-nut straight, unless the ace-high straight is involved. Although a non-nut straight often wins the pot (if the nut holding that beats it was a gut-shot), especially in no-limit or pot-limit Omaha, non-nut straights are of questionable value.

From the standpoint of quality over quantity, the best draws in Omaha are the 16-card all-nuts straight draws. All of these are like the 20-card draws with the top card removed—for example, K Q 10 9, K Q 9 8, A J 10 9, or Q J 10 9 with boards A J 8, A J 10, K Q 8 7, or A K 8 7, respectively. A 16-card all-nut draw may also consist of two separate 8-card nut draws—for example, Q J 6 5 with a board of 10 9 4 3. There are some all-nut 13-card draws, more nut draws than some 20-card draws—for example, 9 8 7 or 9 8 6 with boards of 6 5 or 7 5, respectively.

Straights do win a lot of pots in Omaha, and they are particularly valuable when no flushes or pairs are present. When the flop hits with one high card and an innocuous looking 7 and 6, players betting and raising with top two pair or trips seldom realize that a monster draw like 9 8 5 4 might be lurking and that it will win the pot more than half the time. Even the rather frequent 13-card draws (9 8 5, for example) will make a straight about half the time, with two cards to go. Whenever there are a lot of callers and the flop hits with three cards that do not make a straight but are fairly proximate in rank, you should include the possibility of a big draw in your planning.

## CLOSE TO THE HORNS

How do you feel about making brash big move raises in Omaha? For example, let's say you're playing $10/$20 Omaha with four players contending and about $200 in the pot. The last card counterfeits your nut low, and you now hold a third-rate low and the lowest flush as there are no pairs are on board. The player in front of you lead bets $20, he probably has you beat at least one way. Do you curse your luck and fold? Do you make a fishy call? Or do you make the big move, the double-promo raise on the theory that if the other two players fold you might win half the pot?

Whenever both directions are not locked, raising has much better prospects than calling. Your raise often causes slightly better hands than yours—in both directions—to fold. Instead of playing both ends against the middle, here you are playing the middle against both ends! For more on these high-wire acrobatics see the section called "Big Moves at High-Low," in Chapter 9.

If you make the big move raise, you are investing $40 or even $60 to win $100. Scooping the pot is very unlikely. If you have reason to believe that the other two players are likely to fold a raise—for example, when you know that your customers frequently fish along on nothing, especially when it is cheap, or when their previous actions have indicated trips or a busted low like yours—then the double-promo raise would actually have a positive expectation!

If you truly enjoy making this sort of big move and even find it exciting, then you probably play the game more for enjoyment than for profit. If you have more of a solid professional approach, you undoubtedly prefer to avoid these chancy and swingy situations. In many situations, though, the big move raise is actually the optimum action available at that particular moment. Welcome to the world of Omaha high-low!

There are certain situations in Omaha high-low in which the best strategy is to stick your little neck out and gamble! When you are lucky, your gamble works, and you win. When you are unlucky, you lose. Call it an occupational hazard. At least when these big moves fail, you get good PR—assuming that the other fish notice what a risk taker you are!

But be advised that there is a large downside to playing these hands. Even when these bold actions are correct, they rate to show only a small profit when you look at the bigger picture.

It can be very disheartening when you play the hell out of the hand, have a likely victory in sight, and then get unlucky on the last card and lose a fortune. These hands are often very delicate from a decision-making perspective, which means it is easy for you to go wrong, guess wrong, or misread an opponent—and lose a fortune. It is a lot easier to play good solid hands than these "on the brink" hands. And the good hands also rate to show a much larger profit in the long run. Is there a message here?

Note well that you do not want to be in these situations too frequently, if for no other reason than too much exposure lowers your success rate. Obviously these moves work more frequently if you have a solid reputation. Also note that most of these big moves work better against good players than against fish who are calling stations.

The big question is: would you rather make these moves only when forced to by fate or is it good business to promote these situations? How does one go about promoting or avoiding these big-move situations? Is there a relationship between being in these situations and the type of hands that you play? A definite yes!

If you frequently play secondary or what I call **brinky** values—such as low flushes and medium low cards—you often find yourself in these situations. When you play prime values, you tend to avoid many of these situations. **Flop surfing**, seeing the flop with less than adequate hands, with these hands definitely increases the occurrence of big move situations.

Some typical brinky initial starting hands which often result in these risky business situations are 2 4 5 x, 3 4 4 5, and 4 5 5 6. Especially if they're double suited, these hands are marginally playable in a late seat, though I do not recommend them. This type of hand frequently flops a fishy four-flush and an even fishier third-rate low. But, when you're in late seat, and there's light or no betting, these hands often show a small profit! Not your cup of tea?

If you are a professional at Omaha high-low, what is your image? Do you lay back like a predator? Your opponents are essentially paying you money for entertainment, although they do not realize it. Should you just sit there coldly and grind out a living? The above marginal situation could be the key to spicing up your image at little or no cost! Why be just a spectator? Why let the fish have all the fun? Sense the question marks, disdain, and contempt in the eyes of your fellow pros! If you are good—or just lucky—you can actually play and go plus on these brinky hands!

Just do not let your sense of humor make you play these hands too often, because overexposure from making big moves reduces your effectiveness and success rate. How often should you indulge in these marginal activities, if at all? An acceptable frequency might be either when you're defending your blind, but the position is basically wrong, or as an occasional indiscretion when you're in late seat, which is better. As I mentioned before, you can write off all disasters to your PR account.

## THE LAST CARD BLUES
This section is dedicated to the memory of the thousands of winning hands that we have held on fourth street that were no longer winning hands on fifth street and also to the memory of the many dollars that went with them.

If you want to maintain good professional poise at the Omaha table, you must learn to treat the cruelest of last card losses like water off the back of a duck. Developing a flexible sense of humor might help. In any case, when you play Omaha high-low, these unlucky losses will occur frequently! Perhaps the healthiest attitude is that you should expect to get screwed at least several times a session. There is no alternative; you simply must learn to cope.

If you are playing the game correctly, though, you should win more money on last card draws than you lose. This calculation takes into account the fact that a lot of fish are fishing along and beating you out in some hands that they should not even be playing, which, of course, constantly increases the amount you win in your winning hands.

Remember, in Omaha high-low, there are a lot of hands where it is quite correct to fish along, simply calling, until the last card. Players who play too tight are not optimizing their winning possibilities. The real skill is to be able to know the difference between investing on good odds and fishing along on bad odds. It is often correct to call and see the fourth card—and then drop if you do not hit. If the value is there, put up your money and take your chances. In the long run you should come out ahead—as long as you are figuring things right.

But Omaha high-low can be a very frustrating game since, as we have mentioned, the bi-directionality complicates your evaluation of opponents hands and actions. And, as a result, you all too often find yourself in a large pot where pure luck dominates and skill takes the back seat. And you can lose a lot!

Because of this danger, it is practical to avoid huge swing situations where luck is a big factor. Since there is a large last-card luck factor in Omaha high-low, the better players would be well advised to keep most big pots about the same size—except when they have a lock or are a huge favorite.

Thus, when the pot gets to a normal, good size, the better player might choose to ease up on pot building if he's running on thin percentages. This is also an argument against making too many extra raises which are not likely to drop anyone. To put it another way, if most of the pots are roughly the same size, the good players are less likely to lose the big one—and the last card blues will hurt less.

*Answer to quiz question: The 20-card draw beats the top set about 56% of the time.*

# 6 GOING HIGH

## GOING HIGH AT HIGH-LOW

At four-card Omaha, you can expect to pick up four high cards slightly less than 4% of the time. Computer simulations indicate that these four-high-card starting hands at Omaha high-low actually win less than an average share of the hands. For example, against four random opponents, typical high card hands such as A Q J 10, K Q J 10 and K Q 10 9 win only about 17% of the time, less than the average expected win of 20% with five players in the pot, when low is possible. When low is impossible, however, hands with all four cards 9s or higher are playable because they show a nice profit on one-way high flops.

How often does a high flop occur? About one-fourth of the time. Two high cards and one low card flop about 22% of the time; all three high cards flop about 3% of the time. Note that it is important to have all four of your cards be 9s or higher since your game plan usually is to play only after a high flop. If you hold one low card with three high cards, that one low card usually detracts from your overall winning percentages by lessening your **depth**, the capability of winning with a Plan B or Plan C, and often renders your hand unprofitable mathematically.

It may help your overall perspective if you understand that playing a four high-card starting hand at Omaha high-low is very much a good news/bad news situation. The bad news is that when two low cards hit the flop, low makes about three-fourths of the time. When low is odds-on, investing in most high hands is unprofitable—especially in a volatile game. Even top set has a dubious expectation if two aggressive low hands with potential high holdings jack up the stakes.

The good news is that when you do get a high flop—about one quarter of the time—the value of your high-oriented starting hand increases significantly because:

**1.** You are quite likely to have a piece of the flop or have enough secondary potential to see the fourth card.

**2.** There is considerably more money in the starting pot than in a similar straight Omaha high pot. This is because of the low-hand contributions to the before-the-flop betting.

**3.** In most loose Omaha high-low games, some of the low hands will fish in with inadequate values, thus adding even more money to the pot.

In a loose Omaha high-low game, if you have a high-card hand and you get a two high-card-one-low-card flop, it is absolutely critical that someone bets to chase out the low hands before they see the fourth card.

If the pot was raised before the flop, and thus the size of the starting pot is increased, one of the high hands should raise after the flop. Otherwise, some of the low hands might have enough secondary values to call a single bet and see the fourth card.

Let's look at a typical hand. You hold K♠ Q♥ J♠ 9♦. Six players, including the blinds, see the flop. The flop comes Q♠ 10♥ 5♣. Note that almost any two high cards give you some prospects here. Both blinds check, the player in front of you bets, and it is your turn. You should raise! You have a pair of queens and a big wrap. But straights are very fragile in Omaha! You want to narrow the field. Your raise not only forces out possible lows (with one low card in the flop, low makes about one fourth of the time), but also increases the pressure on possible full houses and backdoor flushes. You want as little competition as possible to win the present pot, and you would be delighted if everyone folded.

If you get heads up, your pair of queens may be a factor. Note that even if you get lucky and hit a straight on your next card (you have seventeen outs), there will still be the usual 40%+ chance of a flush or full house on the river, but your raise might have made the opponent who would have held it fold.

Just after the flop, if the pot contains six bets plus the lead bettor's bet, and one other player and the lead bettor call your raise, there will be twelve units in the pot. Since you'll hit your big-wrap straight over 60% of the time (with two cards coming), you rate to win the hand around half the time against few opponents. Thus your thinning the field raise is clearly justified.

The following three principles may help you do better in straight high situations:
• Keep it cheap before the flop, one-way high hands are average-minus until you get a high flop.
• Fold most high-only hands if two or three low cards flop.
• Play very aggressively after a high flop, and divvy up the dead low money.

Since most experts agree that straight high Omaha is a much more skill-oriented game than Omaha high-low, it follows that there is much skill involved in playing these high-only situations. And usually, the most opportune time to bluff at Omaha high-low is in a straight high situation.

## DRIVING HIGH AT HIGH-LOW OMAHA

Now that we've discussed the realities of playing a high-only hand at loose Omaha high-low, let's follow through and talk about what to do after a high flop. If you are playing a high-only hand at loose Omaha high-low, and you are fortunate enough to have a high flop hit the table, your strategy is amazingly simple. Most of the time and with most hands, you bet—especially if there is one low card in the flop, it is critical to get the low hands out or make them pay to draw for a backdoor low.

How good does your hand have to be to bet? Almost any high stuff will do! Since it is likely that you have the only hand with four high cards, you probably have the best high potential, relative to hands with some low cards, even if you are not ahead at the moment. You probably have at least one high pair and some straight or flush equities. At this point the simple fact that you have four high cards puts you in position to bet—if only to see how the other players respond.

You want to be in the advantageous position of seizing the initiative and becoming the driver. Because it is both strategically and tactically correct to do this, it is not a question of "to drive or not to drive." The only question at all is, "Is there any good reason *not* to drive?" Perhaps the most important winning advice my earlier book on Omaha gives is to drive high hands instead of calling. Driving aggressively not only helps you steal an occasional hand, but it also gets you more callers on your good hands and helps give you a very positive image.

There are a number of reasons for aggressively betting a high flop at Omaha high-low with any pure high hand after the flop. First, and most important, is the one I mentioned above: if there is a low card in the flop, you want to make the low hands fold or pay. Second, and also very important, you want to improve your chances of winning by driving out players who might outdraw you if they're given a free card. How many times have you wished you had stayed in when the fourth card turned? Third, since you should have well above average chances of winning, you would like to get more money into these pots. Although it might sometimes seem that you would rather not put more money into a pot until you see the next card (for example, with a good draw), you do not want to risk winning a nothing pot if you hit, and you might back in with a lesser holding. Given that you have four high cards with a high flop, think more rather than less.

Often there is a delicate balance between saving your money and investing money to make the pot look healthy in case you hit. This first after-the-flop bet often serves the purpose of turning what might have been a nothing pot into a something pot. If it really is destined to be a nothing pot, then you might as well bet and pick up the antes now. At the least, you'll narrow the action before somebody else improves and becomes a contender.

A fourth reason for betting the flop is the strategic advantage in being the bettor. There is always some chance that everyone will fold and you will be an instant winner, though that's somewhat rare at Omaha. If that doesn't happen, you have put in no more money than the callers, and you have seized the initiative. If you and the other callers are all on draw hands and no one hits, then whoever makes the final bet will probably win a reasonable pot, unchallenged. We have all seen hands where several callers have all essentially conceded after seeing the final card—even before the driver made his final drive bet. Take what they are willing to give you.

There are also several image-related strategic reasons for betting the flop and then following through by exercising your option of driving on fourth and fifth streets. Aggressive driving, if not overdone, has a direct effect on several of your psychological image areas, such as your "love" image, where you get to paint one sledge hammer on your sleeve for each hand you drive successfully, your response factor, which directly effects the tightness or the looseness of your callers, and the control factor, when players are consciously or subconsciously competing to dominate the game.

To complete this study, let's take one more look at driving from the negative point of view—that is, what happens when you do *not* drive. You do not beat on your chest and proclaim to the world that you are proud of your hand. Instead you check—perhaps ferociously with a mean look in your eye. Most likely someone else will bet and you have enough to call. But now you are a caller. You have lost the vim of being the driver.

Are you thinking that if you check and someone else bets, you are now in position to check raise? Creative thinking—but that won't work with a medium hand. Since the bettor was in later position than you, a check raise accomplishes nothing! And you probably don't want to put more of your money into a pot at this juncture, especially when you are out-positioned.

Thus, if you fail to drive when you should, you are throwing away some of your present winning percentages as well as potential future ("lovable image") profits. There is a common tendency for new Omaha players to sit back and merely call with some excellent draws like four-to-a-nut-flush or a multi-card straight. This practice perhaps reflects their "bird-in-hand" training, which is often correct in seven stud. Note that if the other players are similarly disposed, it is probably a rather tight, dull game, and this particular pot may well get checked around. Are you able to see what's wrong with that picture?

Just because you should drive after the flop automatically does not mean that you will continue to drive on fourth street, at the larger size bet limit, especially if a scary card turns. You must learn to be very sensitive to signs that advise you to stop driving, particularly on fourth street. And there are certain one shot type hands which you did not plan to bet on fourth street unless they improved; this is the case with most combination hands. There is no dishonor in a quick retreat and a prudent fold.

If conditions look favorable, though, you might continue driving and try the bluff. Whether you continue your driving campaign depends on three main factors: the quality of your driving hand, the fourth street card, and, mostly, the competition remaining. As you gain experience, hopefully you will learn to distinguish when it is best to follow through with a bluff drive—certainly no more than a third of the time—or when it is best to stop driving and conserve your losses.

Aggressive driving is the simple answer to the question; what do you do after a high flop? The only situations in which you don't drive are those in which you have an excellent hand and you detect a pulling opportunity—that is, you want to pull in certain fish or set up some high level ploy (such as letting a "designated bettor" type do the betting). You can drive too frequently at straight high Omaha. At Omaha high-low, though, the high number of driving opportunities, both high-hand and high-flop, makes overdriving unlikely.

## PUSHING A HIGH FLOP

In Omaha high-low, when there are two or three high cards in the flop, low is either unlikely—about 5 to 1 against with one low card in the flop—or impossible. There are significant differences between Omaha high-low with a high flop and straight high Omaha. In Omaha high-low, most of the players seeing the flop probably have low cards, and the starting pot has been enlarged by their contributions.

Thus, when you have a high-oriented hand at Omaha high-low and you get a high flop, you are substantially better off than when you hold that same hand at Omaha straight high. Not only is the starting pot larger (thus offering better odds), but also the competition rates to be less formidable. Clearly this affects your strategy. At Omaha high-low, when you have a high hand after a high flop, it is often correct to be very aggressive—even if you hit the flop only partially.

How often do you get a high flop? If you deal three random cards from a fifty-two card deck, two or three cards will be 9 or higher (not including aces) almost one-third of the time. If you are looking at four hand cards all 9 or higher, there will be two or three high cards in the flop only about one-fourth of the time.

When you have a straight high hand and get a high flop, what do you need to bet the flop? Perhaps the best answer is that all you need is good high potential. It's definitely a push hard situation. Even if you have a **high plus hand**—that is, three high cards including an ace and one low card (here the ace sometimes makes an **emergency low** which might salvage half the pot—your strategy almost always is to push. You certainly do not want to check it out and let the low hands see a second low card.

Suppose you hold a pure high hand such as K J J 10 in five- or six-way action and flop a K 9 6. Three or four of the opposing hands are usually low-card oriented. Although you have merely a pair of kings and a gut straight draw, you should consider betting in any seat. Your bet should eliminate most of the low hands or make them play at bad odds. Even a slight possibility of everyone folding (for example, perhaps one time in seven), tends to justify your bet, and thus betting is much better than calling.

Another frequent occurrence is that you get one or two feeble callers who fold after the fourth card. Unless you run into an opponent who has a good hand has flopped a set or top two pair—and raises, you have not cost yourself much money. With almost any four high-card hand and two unpaired high cards in the flop, you should have some chances of hitting a good card and winning.

Because you have good high potential, your actual odds of ending up with the best hand must be significantly better than average. I simulated the above hand using Mike Caro's Poker Probe against four and five opponents. I constrained two of the hands to hold an A2 and a 2 3 5, which are typical calling hands. Whenever you have five or six callers, even in a loose game, there usually will be a couple of A2 A3 23 holdings. The simulation indicated that the K J J 10 hand won about one-third of the time against four opponents. It obviously outperformed the low hands and won almost twice as often as the random hands.

I simulated various other marginal high hands (for example, A Q J 9 with a flop of K Q 5) and obtained similar results. Thus, whenever no opponent has a good hand with the given flop, pushing the marginal hand is an excellent investment. My experience in these situations is that someone holds a good hand less than half of the time. Thus, the bottom line is that you should make a nice profit if you're aggressive in these situations. But it certainly helps if you know when to back off and avoid big losses.

Don't be overly aggressive on every high flop—it's unwise to become predictable. It also helps if you have a generally tight image carried over from your participation in the two-way hands. My rule-of-thumb is to let the cards decide when I should make a move. If I have at least a high pair *and* a flush or straight draw, I usually bet—unless there are specific players in the pot who affect my strategy. One final caveat: remember that a loose bet after the flop does not commit you to the rest of the hand!

## SPECULATING AFTER A HIGH FLOP

In straight high Omaha, if you have merely the high pair on board and no other values, it is seldom correct to lead bet after the flop. Indeed, you would almost never call a bet with just the high pair, except perhaps in a one-on-one bluff situation. In high Omaha, there are many flops on which it is unwise to lead even with the top two pair. You might think that you should play even more conservatively in Omaha high-low since the high hand often gets only half of the pot. Actually, in Omaha high-low, it is often correct to push a high pair—especially in late seat!

In Omaha high-low, the majority of callers very likely have two-way or low oriented hands. Even in relatively loose games, inferior low-card hands are usually more popular than inferior high-card hands. Next time you are in a **family pot**, one with many callers, take a survey of as many hands as you can. Usually there are some A 2 3-type hands, several mixed and often fishy low or medium hands, and perhaps one or two good high-card hands.

Whenever there is a high flop, most low hands become worthless. Even with one low card in the flop, the best low hands will make an 8 or better low less than one-fourth of the time. What do you do with a high pair if the betting after the flop is checked around to you? If you bet, usually more than half of the hands will fold. If there is a 10-20% chance that everyone will fold, that alone justifies the bet. If you get one or two callers, quite often they will fold if you continue to bet. Add those prospects to the possibility that you might have or draw the best hand, and it seems clear that driving a high pair is actually a winning proposition—especially if you do it infrequently.

How often will a hand with a high pair on the flop win high? Assuming that many of the players will fold mixed hands, such as two high or medium cards and two lower but not prime low cards, before the flop, then your high pair is slightly better at high-low than at straight high because you have less high card competition. Since many of the hands that call to see the flop are predominately low hands, whenever there is a high flop, it is imperative that a high hand bets so that most of these low hands will fold! The remaining high hands then compete for a considerably larger pot than there would have been at straight high—which greatly affects the odds of the situation. Note that some high hands, even those that are slightly better than yours, will often fold the bet, and that also improves your odds.

If you are acting in a late position, the odds of running into a big high hand, trips or top two, for example, are substantially less if no one has bet in front of you. Most players know it is bad economics to trap with a good high hand—it might cost half the pot if the lows get a free second low card. If someone raises, you might choose to get out cheaply. When you play in the fast lane, it helps to know your competition.

The following example illustrates some typical percentages. Suppose you call in late seat with A 3 of spades, a queen and a 7. The flop comes Q 10 4 offsuit, and it gets checked around to you. I ran the following hands (note two high hands and only two low hands) 100,000 times on Mike Caro's Poker Probe. The two low hands should fold a bet after the flop, and the pair of kings might fold. If you were playing against only the 9 9 10 J (or most draws), you would win high well over 50% of the time. Take a look at the chart below (underlined cards are suited).

| Hand | Winning % (including low) |
|---|---|
| A 2 6 8 | 8.83 |
| K K 8 6 | 13.64 |
| 2 3 5 7 | 9.28 |
| J T 9 9 | 29.67 |
| RANDOM (blind) | 16.38 |
| A 3 Q 7 | 22.14 |

Note that the random blind hand rates to be stronger competition than the low-card hands. Whenever you bet with marginal cards and with medium board cards, you root for the blinds to fold. You cannot really judge what you might encounter in a random hand. If you do get one or two callers, there is no clear recommendation as to what you do next  as it's usually an opponent-dependent situation. Against some opponents, peacefully checking is superior to driving, which is cheaper.

In summary, the main points for betting after the flop are:
• You either fold the low competition or make them pay more than their low chances are worth
• You might fold all the competition
• You might fold some marginal (even better than you) high competition
• Overall, betting should increase your chances of winning the pot, perhaps by as much as 20% or more, regardless of how you choose to follow through

That certainly fully justifies your after-the-flop investment.

## WHAT WINS AT OMAHA

Before reading the next paragraph, you might test your insight and perception of high and high-low Omaha by asking yourself the following questions:
• What percentage of high hands is won with full houses?
• What percentage of hands is won with flushes?
• What percentage of hands is won with straights?
• What percentage of hands is won with hands lower than straights?

I once estimated that about one-fourth of high hands are won by each of the above four categories. Surprisingly, that estimate was quite accurate! Knowing what wins at Omaha should improve your overall perspective of the game. It might also improve your before-the-flop strategy.

There are no exact answers to these questions—the situation depends on the number of players and the looseness or tightness of the game. Computer simulations (using Mike Caro's Poker Probe) with from two to ten random players playing each hand to completion indicate that the percentage of hands won with straights (about 24% with four players to 27% with ten players) and flushes (about 18% with four players to 22% with ten players) fluctuates considerably less as the number of players varies than does the full house win percentage (about 20% with four players to 36% with ten players).

Judging from the computer-generated percentages for four to six players, which roughly approximate real playing conditions with many hands folding, the winning hand percentages seem to be about 25% for straights, 20% for flushes, 25% to 30% for full houses, and the remainder won with lower hands (mostly trips or two pair). Four-of-a-kind wins only about one-half percent (.00475) times the number of players. In real life, flushes seem to win slightly more often than 20% of the time, perhaps because some hands that might win with a full house fold before the showdown.

As expected, Caro's Poker Probe generates the same high hand results at Omaha high-low as at high Omaha (with no folding). It is unclear if playing more low-oriented hands in real-life Omaha high-low produces any significant difference in the high hand win mix, except that with more players playing until the showdown at Omaha high-low than at high Omaha, a slightly larger percentage of full houses might win high.

All in all, these numbers tend to verify that high pocket pairs are the most valuable two-card high holdings (as reflected in my point count system) since full houses, trips, and two pairs win over half of all hands. But since flushes and straights win almost half of the hands, it is also critical to play starting hands with high suited cards and **proximate**, that is straight-making, cards to contend for that half of the pie.

Thus, the very best high starting hands in Omaha are well-balanced or coordinated with one or two high pairs, once- or twice-suited, and proximate high cards. Hands which contain all of these, sometimes get a flop with all three working! For example, if you hold an ace, a king, and two queens, you might flop a queen, jack and 10 with the nut-flush draw! How sweet it is to face the last-card roulette with most of the numbers covered!

## FLUSHING AT HIGH-LOW

Say you're playing ten-handed Omaha high-low. You flop the nut flush draw, you hold ace and another of a suit and the flop has two cards of that suit and no pair. What factors determine whether you normally check or bet, call or raise, keeping in mind that sometimes you depart from normal strategy?

The nut flush draw is naturally a pulling hand. You want more opponents in the pot to increase your payoff if you hit. You also would rather not increase your investment until you hit, since you make your flush only about 35% of the time with two cards coming, and about 20% of the time on the last card. So the most normal actions are to check instead of bet, call instead of raise.

Omaha high-low, however, is hardly a normal game; you often take seemingly abnormal actions. Since there is a split pot about half of the time, your normal strategy is strongly influenced by the number of low cards in the flop.

If the flop contains three high cards, there will be no low. You check your flush draw in early seats and let the straights do the betting. In last seat or if the pot was raised before the flop, you might bet, unless you judge that there is no chance that everyone will fold. If you bet and get one or two callers, you might continue to drive bluff if you don't hit.

If the flop contains two high cards and one low card, then you might bet on the theory that one of the high hands has to bet to keep the lows out since a free fourth card may cost you half a pot when you win high. You are more anxious to bet if you hold a bad low draw yourself. If you have the nut two-card low draw, then you certainly do not bet, because you want the low guys in more than you want them out. With high flops, if there is an early-seat bet and you are in a late seat, you usually make the inhibitory raise, which tends to get the betting checked around to you after the fourth card which then gives you the option of getting a free last card.

If the flop contains two low cards, you have no reason to increase the stakes, unless you happen to have some mediocre two-way possibilities in addition to your nut flush draw. You might raise (rather than call) after the flop if you judge that the raise will create great pressure on opponents to fold marginal lows and promote your lesser holdings into contention.

Note that with certain marginal holdings it is often right to make an immediate after-the-flop probing raise, when the opportunity presents itself or perhaps a promo raise, rather than just to call, assuming your cards warrant pushing. When you're playing Omaha high-low, you often encounter the great comedian's sister, Raisin Hope. And remember the words found inscribed on the pyramid, "'Tis far better to be the jerkor than the jerkee."

No jerking with a nut-flush or nut low draw, though! The probing raise, which is most effective in a tightish high-low game when you have a marginal two-way call after the flop and there are several players yet to act behind you, is not advisable here, since with the probing raise, unless your hand improves significantly, you tend to fold on the next round if there are several callers. When you have the nut flush draw, usually you are **stuck in** until the last card, and thus a probing raise must be wrong because the information is less useful, it costs money, and you *want* more callers if you hit. Simply put, it is usually wrong to push in a pulling situation.

If three low cards flop and you do not have a nut low, check and call and try to keep things cheap. Since you can win only half a pot if you hit, you may have to fold this hand rather than play a capped-out after fourth card round. Sometimes you do get trapped in, though. On rare occasions when there is too big a starting pot to fold and you are "stuck in" until the last card unless the board pairs), you might join in the raising after the flop to fake a nut low and attempt to keep the betting down on the next round. If you are sitting in last chair, and the pot happens to get checked around to you, you might bet to promote mediocre two-way holdings, and perhaps get it checked around to you on the next round.

You should not lose sight of the fact that the nut flush draw, by itself, is less than half as valuable when there is a likely low split. Taken in combination with other holdings, though, it often adds enough value to a hand to make aggressive playing a better option than calling or folding.

## HIGH-ONLY HANDS AT HIGH-LOW

Most of the Omaha high-low games that you find today are of the loose variety. Once again, my definition of loose is a game in which more than five players on average are seeing the flop. One of the starting hand types that I recommend playing at loose Omaha high-low is the high-only hand. This hand is best when all four of your cards are 9s or higher.

At Omaha high-low, low cards can win high, but high cards cannot win low. A high-only hand cannot be a favorite if there are two or three low cards in the flop. Since an ace is a low card, there are eight low-making denominations and only five high cards. Mathematically, a three-card flop will contain two or three high cards slightly less than one-third of the time—but only one-fourth of the time if you are looking at four high cards.

When there are two or three high cards in the flop, high-only hands can be very profitable if the starting pot has been enlarged by a number of low-oriented hands, especially if those lows continue to compete. These high-flop situations usually result in no low, of course, which means only one winner. This is called a **scoop**. So, at loose Omaha high-low, even if you hit a high flop only one out of four times, you will still show a nice profit if you scoop a few medium-sized pots.

Tight-aggressive Omaha high-low, which is often played for higher stakes, is dramatically different from loose Omaha high-low. In tight-aggressive Omaha high-low, there typically is a raise before the flop and zero, one, or two callers. It is much like the hard serve and rush-the-net mentality you'll find in high stakes hold 'em.

When there are only a few players seeing the flop—as is the case in tight Omaha high-low—high-only hands are usually *not* cost-effective. Similarly, in shorthanded Omaha high-low play, such as in the final stages of a tournament, most high-only hands are not favorites to win a showdown. I have seen many otherwise good Omaha high-low players apparently misevaluate these high-only hands at tight Omaha high-low.

At a recent Omaha high-low tournament, when there were three players remaining on my big blind, one player raised before the flop with a K Q J 9 holding. I defended my blind with an A 9 6 5. At straight high Omaha, his hand would be a slight favorite over mine. Can you estimate which hand was better and by approximately how much at Omaha high-low?

When these two hands were simulated my hand won roughly 62% of the time! Thus, the ace-plus-low-cards hand was about a 24% favorite over the high-only hand!

In the actual hand, an 8 and a 7 hit in the flop; that put me in excellent position to win the whole pot. Then a 5 turned, which gave me a straight (and a low). Unfortunately, he hit the miracle 10 on the last card—his only card to salvage half the pot—which gave him a higher straight than mine. So we split it. But although he was lucky on that particular hand, I clearly had the best of it.

That hand reminded me of a hand I once encountered in the final stages of a Casino San Pablo Tournament when I resisted the temptation to invest my last few chips in a K Q J 10 hand. Instead, I patiently waited for an ace-and-low-card type of hand. Knowing not to waste my last few chips to play the K Q J 10 hand turned out to be very consequential, because if I had played that hand, I wouldn't have finished in the money in that event, and I wouldn't have won the Player of the Tournament Rolex watch.

So one valuable lesson is that most high-only hands are actually below-average hands at shorthanded Omaha high-low! If you simulate a K Q J 10 (single-suited) hand against a random hand, the random hand wins over 55% of the time! And most high-only hands are *inferior* to random hands by more than ten percentage points! Thus, at tight Omaha high-low, where you seldom get long odds on your investments, you usually do not want to play high-only hands.

What about high-only hands with a high pocket pair? If pocket aces are good, aren't pocket kings almost as good? The short answer is, "No." One reason pocket aces are very good is that the ace also is the best low card.

Do you know that pocket kings, a queen, and a jack, unsuited, is an slight underdog to a random hand at head-to-head Omaha high-low? If one of the kings is suited (with the queen or jack), that hand is about a 51% winner against a random hand. Note that against three doggy-looking low cards, such as an 8, a 6 and a 4, unsuited, that pocket kings high hand is over a five percent underdog! Such is the nature of Omaha high-low.

Before you play a high-only hand, look around and judge whether you will have enough company to keep the percentages on your side (I prefer four-way action or more). And remember: thou shall usually fold if there are two low cards in the flop. Amen.

## EXAMPLE OF PUSHING HIGH

Say you're playing loose Omaha high-low. You're in the next-to-last seat, and you pick up A♠ 4♠ 2♥ 9♥. In addition to the blinds, three players call around to you. With the A 2 4 in a well-attended pot, you make the automatic raise before the flop. You don't mind when the button folds, since that gives you last position, which is a nice advantage. Everyone else calls.

Now you're in six-way action, and once again your dreams of low cards are dashed when Q♦ 9♠ 6♥ hits the flop. However, it is checked around to you. Do you graciously accept the free card?

I didn't. I think this hand has enough all-around potential to bet and put some pressure on the checkers, even though it is quite possible that you might run into a check-raiser. It is important *not* to give the checkers a free card—that might lead to their beating you out of half a pot or even the whole pot. For example, if the next card is a heart, someone might have two hearts higher than yours. The next card could also give someone trips.

I bet in last seat, and one of the blinds check-raised. Everyone else folded. I had noticed that the check-raiser was the real "operator" type and quite aggressive. Obviously, I planned at least to call. Since I was sitting behind him, though, I thought I'd "test him out" by reraising (which might get me the option of having a free last card). He thought about it and fiddled with his chips. I was almost expecting "the reluctant reraise," but he just called.

The fourth card was the 4♥—a pretty good card for me. It gave me two (low) pair, a nut low draw, and a heart flush draw. But he came out betting. Maybe he really had something? All I could do was call.

The last card was the J♥. Overall, I liked it—though I would rather have had an emergency low in reserve. He bet. Did he have a higher flush than mine? Ace-other of hearts was the nuts. Not likely. Would you call or raise?

I merely called. He had nothing but a pair of 9s (king-high). His hand was K 9 8 7. So if I had raised he would have folded. Two of the problems with raising are:

- If he has you beat, instead of winning twenty extra dollars, you will probably lose forty, since this guy was the type of player that you have to call in limit poker.
- He might drop your raise—thus you have risked raising for nothing.

Note that there are a lot of "ifs" in a hand like this. What would have happened if the last card had been a do-nothing card and he had bet? Although my pair of 9s, ace-high, had him beat, I might have folded.

## EXAMPLE OF RAISING HIGH

I normally would prefer pot-limit Omaha—though not knowing the players is a tremendous disadvantage. On my first visit to the Biloxi Grand's poker room the first available seat was in $10/$20 Omaha high-low. With six to eight (!) players seeing every flop, I knew I had found a home. Two kibitzers asked me several questions about my raising after the flop at Omaha high-low; I will pass my comments on to you.

After playing two rounds and having thrown away most starting hands, in second seat I called with A♠ 10♠ Q♣ 4♥. With a total of six callers, the flop came J♠ 10♥ 7♦. The first player, who had previously bet every time it was his turn, bet the flop. I could feel the question marks in my kibitzer's heads as I raised! Three players folded, and there were three players remaining. Unfortunately, a jack turned, and I folded the lead bet.

Shortly thereafter, both kibitzers wanted to know why I had raised with that pitiful holding. I explained that my raise was partly an image builder—the type of raise that I often make early in a new environment. With a fairly large starting pot and two high cards on the flop, it was not unreasonable for me to call and compete. But if I was good enough to call, why not invest one more bet to put the pressure on any other marginal callers and gut-straight drawers. Since the lead flop bettor was known to bet on sketchy values, it was unlikely that he had the 8 9 nuts. My raise tended to show the 8 9 or perhaps a set, I had already acquired a tight image—if anyone had noticed, and it would leave me well-placed to steal the pot later. On a good day I might even draw my nut-straight or backdoor a low or a flush.

Another very important strategic consideration was that my after-the-flop raise, in conjunction with later after-the-flop raises that I would make would tend to program my opponents and get them used to calling my pushy raises after the flop. I play very aggressively after the flop, and so should you in push situations because in Omaha, I would rather be loved than feared. Note that if there had been two spades in the same flop, I would not have raised to push out a player with two small spades who might otherwise fish in.

A few rounds later, holding A K J 3, I raised the same lead bettor after the flop hit with a J 9 5 offsuit. Again there were three players, and a 6 turned. Note that my raise after the flop might have caused an A 2 holding that might have "taken one off" at half the price to fold. The previous lead bettor checked to me; it seemed right to bet. The third player called, and the lead bettor folded. The last card was another 6. We both checked, and my jack-ace won the pot because he was drawing for a high straight. I had won another typical **nothing pot**—which is critical to success at Omaha high-low.

So here's a tip: when you're playing loose Omaha high-low, when two or more high cards hit the flop, it is often better to raise, especially with position, than to call with marginal holdings.

## CAPPELLETTI OMAHA POINT COUNT SYSTEM (for High Omaha)

In order to calculate the sum of the two-card combinations, I have quantified the results of my research into a relatively simple point count system for evaluating the flop potential of the initial four cards at Omaha. This point count system assigns a certain number of points to each of the six two-card combinations. The points assigned to each combination are added together. If the total equals eleven or more, I recommend calling. If the total exceeds sixteen, I recommend raising.

However, as always, this is all subject to the game and your position. You might want to raise or call with fewer points to loosen up a tight game, in games where the before-the-flop bet is less than one-half of the maximum bet ($2/$5 or $10/$20/$30), or simply because you are in last betting position. If you are playing in a game where the before-the-flop betting is extremely vigorous and is often capped, you should tighten up on your initial calls.

If you are playing three-card Omaha, in which there are only three two-card combinations, not six two-card combinations as in four-card Omaha, I recommend calling with a total of six points or more and raising with ten points or more. Admittedly, my point count system is not as accurate in three-card Omaha (for example, pairs and lesser flush holdings should be given at least one extra point).

There are three categories of two-card pairs for which I give points. In addition, there are individual high-card bonuses and position bonuses. The point count system is detailed below.

## CAPPELLETTI OMAHA POINT COUNT
## SYSTEM (for two-card combinations)

Pairs:   Points = Denomination/2 + 2
      e.g.    two aces = 14/2 + 2 = 9 points
               two queens = 12/2 + 2 = 8 points
               two 5s = 5/2 + 2 = 5 points

Flushes:     (x = any card in same suit)
             A x = 6 points
             K x = 5 points
             Q x = 3 points
             J x = 2 points
             x x = 1.5 points

Straights:    2 touching cards = 2 points
              (excluding A 2 and 2 3)
              (exception: J 10 = 3 points)
             2 cards missing one = 2 points
              (excluding A 3)
              (exception: 2 4 = 1 point)
             2 cards missing two = 1 point
              (excluding A 4)
             Third card bonus = 2 points
              (but not A or 2)
             Fourth card bonus = 2 points
              (within five pips)

High Card Bonus:  (don't give this extra bonus to paired cards)
                      Aces thru 10s—1 point each
                      9s thru 7s—1/2 point each

Position Bonus: 2 points for last; 1 point for next to last

A few examples:
A K A K (both suited) = 9+9+6+6+2 = 32 (best hand)
Q J 10 9 = 2+2+1+3+2+2 +2+2+3+1/2 = 19+ (both suited=24)
J 9 8 6 = 2+1+2+1+2 +2+2+1+1 = 14
A Q 9 8 = 2+1+2 +2+2+1 = 10
J 8 6 4 = 1+2+2 +2+1+1/2 = 8+

Note that aces and face cards are given extra points in their straight points, that is more than their actual straight potential merits. For example, an AK gets 2 points, which is more than it merits for its straight potential but is about right considering the AK overall high card potential value. Thus the true value of high cards is reflected in points by using the high card bonus added to this inflated straight point bonus.

Pairs are the best two-card holdings, since they flop a set (trips) about one out of eight times—slightly more often than two flush cards flop a four-flush. Although low sets can be dangerous, everyone I know would like to have more of them. Even a low pair leads to a win more frequently than an A X suited—although the flush is more likely to be the nuts.

Most players tend to over-value the A X suited holding, though it *is* one of the better holdings, since it leads to a direct lock-flush win about one out of twenty-one pots. Lower flush cards are seriously demoted for their second-best potential. However dangerous they are, low flushes sometimes do back into big pots, and they certainly add a tangible equity to other playable holdings.

The 2-point bonus for a third proximate card and 2 additional points for a fourth proximate card reflect the advantages of flops with more than eight straight-hit cards (nine to twenty!) For example, when you hold J 9 8 6, a 10 7 flop gives you twelve straight-hit cards, and all of the straights are nut straights.

The reason one-hole straight holdings, for example, 8 6 are given the same two points as two touching cards like 8 7, is that for flopping purposes, both holdings give two "good" open-end four-straights. Note that only the J 10 holding has three good four straights. Take a look:

- 8 6 is good when you flop 9 7 or 7 5 (eight hit cards)
- 8 7 is good when you flop 9 6 or 6 5
- 10 9 is not good (on low end)
- J 10 is good with Q 9, 9 8, or K Q—thus it gets 3 points.

# 7 LET'S PLAY SOME HANDS

The bad news is that a cruel last card had cost me a possible win at Atlantic City's Tropicana's "last Friday of the month $200 buy-in" hold 'em tournament. The good news is that I had $1792 for coming in third in my pocket as I took a seat in a live $10-$20 Omaha high-low game.

On my first hand, I posted two red chips behind the button. I picked up J 8 8 2, a hand we would all normally fold. No one raised. It was five-way action, and the flop came 8 6 2 offsuit. There were three checks to me. Although top set is seriously devalued with three low cards since high gets only half the pot and the low cards might straighten, I bet. The button folded, and the other three players called. Thus, I was now in four-way action.

The fourth card was the king of spades, the second spade. My opponents checked around to me. Hoping to get some folds, I bet—but they all called. The last card was the deuce of hearts. Again they checked around to me.

Since my 8s full house was the second nuts, and thus very likely to win high, I bet. One fold, one call, and then the right-hand opponent check-raised! Would you call, hoping to pull in the caller for one more double bet, or raise?

These situations occur often in Omaha high-low. It frequently is correct to call with a one-way lock when you expect to split the pot, especially if it is possible to be tied and get only a quarter of the pot, and you want to pull in one or more opportunistic callers.

Here the opponent on your right is highly unlikely to have the nuts, pocket kings, since he probably would have raised in last calling seat on the previous round. He also is unlikely to be raising at this point with a lock low (A 3), because there's danger of being quartered, especially in light of his earlier calls. Probably, he had just made a full boat, such as deuces over kings, and thought that I was betting a low.

In this situation, note how important it is to raise and try to push out the crawler who might have a dubious low. I reraised, and the caller thought for a moment and then folded the double raise. The check-raiser called with his 6s full and no low! So I scooped the whole pot, while the opponent who had dropped frowned.

Several rounds later, I was in middle seat, and I called with A K Q 10 once-suited. It was six-way action, and the flop came 10 9 2. After two checks, I bet the high flop to see what would happen because almost any four high cards may bet a high flop. Unfortunately, there were four callers. The fourth card was a second deuce. I would have folded any bet. But it was checked all around.

The last card was the useless 5 of spades. It went check around to me. Since no one had bet the fourth card, there was a fair chance that no one held a deuce. In that case, I had a marginal hand in an unwanted pot—and that's a good time to push with a hump bet. The next opponent folded my bet with pocket jacks (he later told me what he had). No one else had my 10s with ace kicker beat. But since it was clearly a lucky night for me, the last opponent gave me a bonus by calling with 10s and queen-high.

Note that the difference between a bluff and a hump bet in an unwanted pot, after a check around, is that a bluff is made with little or no values, whereas a hump bet is made with dubious calling values. Generally, in Omaha high-low, you should be constantly watching for reasonable opportunities to push out a marginal hand which might beat your marginal hand for half the pot, and sometimes the whole pot.

# PLAN D

I was on the button in a delightfully loose $10/$20 Omaha high-low game at the Crystal Park Hotel Casino. There were five callers (and two blinds behind me), and I raised before the flop while holding A♠ 10♠ 8♥ 2♦, since my prospects of winning rated to be almost twice that of most of the other players. Raising before the flop in a loose game not only increases the amount of money in the pot, but also makes it more likely that the fish will put in even more money, often with inadequate cards (which they might have folded with a lesser starting pot).

There was seven-way action, and this time fate presented me with a fine flop: 9♠ 4♠ 6♣, which gave me both a nut-flush draw and a nut low draw.

The betting was checked around toward me, but the player in front of me bet first. With many hands it is right to raise after the flop to force more of the competition to fold and to increase your chances of getting the dead money already in the pot. It is clearly not best to raise, however, when you have super-pot potential.

Winning or splitting little pots is fine when your prospects are not that great or unclear. But what really makes your day at Omaha high-low is scooping up a big one. Constructing a potential big one is, therefore, always my first objective—if I have excellent two-way potential. In one word: you pull instead of push.

On this flop I had nineteen cards (eight spades, three 3s, three 5s, three 7s, and two 8s) that would give me the nuts in at least one direction, and seven cards would give me the two-way nuts (four 7s and the 3, 5, and 8 of spades). Thus, Plan A was to hit one of the double-nut cards. Plan B and Plan C were to hit one of the nut high or nut low cards.

So, hoping to pull in a crowd, I merely called—and indeed there were four more callers. It was six-way action, and the elephant queen of diamonds turned. Apparently no one liked the queen—it was checked around to me. Although I often subscribe to the bird-in-hand philosophy, which is wait until I hit my draw, with seven two-way nut cards, I liked my odds and made the double bet. Only one player folded.

It was now five-way action, and another elephant hit—this time the jack of diamonds. Although this wasn't one of the lock-cards I had been rooting for, it did give me a low-end straight in what was now a one-way high pot. And then it went all check around to me! Although a K 10—the nuts— might be lurking for a check-raise, I couldn't resist making the value bet, especially since my earlier betting made my having a straight seem unlikely. Sure enough, I picked up three callers and scooped enough five-dollar chips to add three more stacks to my pyramid.

Note that had I raised after the flop and made several players fold, I might have won only about half as much money—although my Plan D backdoor straight would have been even more likely to win. Perhaps the dominant principle here is that when you have little or no **default holdings**, something that might win if everybody misses—such as a high pair, and since you have to hit something in order to win either half of the pot, it is usually not cost-effective to raise and force out competition that might well lose money to you if you do hit.

# PUSH OR PULL

In loose Omaha high-low, there are many situations in which it is not clear whether you should raise or merely call—that is, whether you should try to push out opponents or pull them in. Some of these situations occur after the flop, when you have one push holding and one pull holding. For example, say you're in early position, and you hold A♠ Q♠, a 10, and a 3. Five players (including you) see the flop, which is Q♥ 7♠ 3♠. The first player to act, bets. When you're in second seat, do you call or raise? Do you want more players or fewer players?

When you have just a nut-flush draw, you should simply call. By not raising, you will pull in more opponents, get more money into the pot, thus giving you better odds and on less of your money invested, and then have more potential callers if you hit. Raising, presumably to get a free fourth card, usually lowers your odds and improves the dollar expectation of the lead bettor.

When you have only two pair on the flop, you prefer shorthanded play so that your two pair is more likely to stand up. If you belong in the pot after the flop, it is often correct to raise to reduce competition, and also to increase the size of the pot.

Perhaps the decisive factor as to whether to call or raise when you have two conflicting considerations is what you judge as the most likely holding of the lead bettor. In the given hand, if you judge that the lead bettor is pushing a high holding, probably better than your queens and 3s—trips, for example, then you are drawing, and it's clear that you should call.

On the other hand, if the lead bettor is a very tight player who is likely to be betting an A 2, then it is probably correct for you to raise and try to make the competition fold. If everyone folds, in head-to-head play—assuming you keep betting and get called—you will normally win about two-thirds of the chips bet (when simulated against the typical A 2), which means your net win will be about five units on average (if 17 units are in the final pot, 5+4+4+4). If you get one caller, your expectation probably goes up a little if the caller is generally loose, but down if the caller is a tight expert.

If you simply call after the flop, it is difficult to estimate your expectation accurately. This also depends on the looseness of the game, but it is probably less than five units net, since you are more likely to lose and less likely to scoop. All in all, I like the raise here since it either narrows the action or boosts the stakes if you get another caller.

Recently, I was in a classic after-the-last-card "milking" situation in which it is often best simply to call and keep it cheap to pick up one or more loose calls from optimistic or opportunistic opponents. I held a K Q J 9 double-suited in six-handed play; the flop was A♣ K♣ and a 4. Looking at the nut flush draw, I checked in second seat and then called a bet, which resulted in four-way action. The fourth card was a 10, which gave me the nut straight. So I bet in second seat and got the same three callers. The fifth card was the 3♣, which improved my nut straight to the nut flush. Then the usually tight first seat player came to life and bet. Should I now raise with my nut flush or call and try to pull in some money from the other two players?

I thought it was clear to raise, and they both folded, as expected. The first seat player called, showed his nut low (2 5), and sarcastically said, "Nice raise." If I had merely called, we each might have received another unit or two. I resisted the temptation to reply, "Nice bet," since he probably should have checked.

From my perspective, if there was any chance that he was betting a high, it was imperative to raise and force out a low caller who might back into half of the pot. Note that winning the whole pot usually nets about three times more chips than a half pot. On this hand, the whole pot would have netted me eighteen units, instead of five plus the one or two extra units if I called.

On both of these hands, the pushy raise was probably the better play. It seems to me that in Omaha high-low, when there are both pushing and pulling considerations, the better play in most situations is the pushy aggressive one. That's generally true in most forms of poker.

## AT TABLE LEVEL

When you first take a seat in a new Omaha high-low game, you should start keeping track of how many players on average are seeing the flop and how many of those callers tenaciously hang on after the flop. If there are more than five players on average seeing the flop, you know you are playing in a loose game ("Cappelletti's Rule") and that there is money floating around.

I would also advise you to look around and notice what the various players are doing. You'll likely notice that some players are playing too many hands and are frequently fishing in with inadequate cards. You may also notice that some players are looking you over. Generally, at this stage, you divide up all the players in the game into three broad categories—those whom you would like to have in your pots (**fish**), those of whom you should probably be cautious (**fishermen**), and perhaps one or two whom you are unable to classify because of insufficient data. This information is worth money. The more you know about your opponents, the more you will be able to improve your percentages.

In the following example, various occurrences and bits of information enabled me to set up a high-percentage situation. I was playing in a new game, and I finally picked up a hand worth playing—an A 3 5 Q with the ace suited. Since I was in the middle of the pack, I just called into six-way action. A nice flop hit the table: an A 2 4 rainbow, which gave me a wheel. The player on my right, who had a lot of chips and whom I had classified as a probable fisherman, made the lead bet. I called. Raising would be foolish since I wanted as many callers as possible. Two other fish category players limped in.

It was four-way action, and the fourth card turned a queen, which gave me top two pair, although I already had a wheel for high. Again the player in front of me bet, and again, I merely called—because I wanted to pull in the other two players. One called; one folded.

The last card was a jack. Again the lead bettor bet, and again I called, but the last player raised! The lead bettor reraised. At this point I realized that I might be getting quartered, so all I could do was call. Sure enough, the fish had hit the big straight, and the lead bettor and I each had a 3 5 for one-quarter of the pot, which meant roughly breaking even. Just another routine, frustrating hand at Omaha high-low. Then I had to listen to my right-hand opponent accuse me of misplaying by not raising earlier. I thanked him for the advice. I did not bother to accuse him of costing us both money with his optimistic final raise.

With that hand for prelude, several hands later, in first position, the same right-hand opponent raised before the flop. Since I had pocket aces and an otherwise bad hand—a 10 and an 8 with four different suits—I reraised, hoping to narrow the action, so aces would be more effective. The same two players who had called the earlier hand cold-called the three bets, which left the same four-way action.

The flop came K 10 2 offsuit—not particularly good, but any two high cards were much better with my hand than any two low cards. My right-hand opponent bet out and I made what I consider the automatic raise (in this situation, if I am going to call, it must be better to raise). One player folded, the same caller who pulled the miracle big straight in the previous hand called, and the lead bettor reraised! Since I was going to call, I decided to reraise—which capped it.

The caller who had made the big straight folded reluctantly, and then the lead bettor said, "You convinced me," and tossed in his hand! Then he said, "See? I told you—all you have to do to win in this game is raise!" Then he whispered to me that I had trip kings, and that I had given away my hand with the reraise. I again thanked him for his advice.

About an hour later, after I had grabbed two more high-only pots, my right-hand opponent/new friend confided in me that the best way to win in Omaha high-low was to go after high. Several times prior to this, he had raised before the flop, prematurely, with an A 2 hand, which is not recommended in early seat if the raise tends to narrow the action, and then he lost big. After making his astute observation, on the very next hand he confidently raised before the flop.

I was looking at a 6 5 5 3 double-suited. Normally I would throw this hand away in third seat in a loose game, although it does play well at head-to-head. But because I suspected he was going high, and since I had reraised after the flop on the previous hand, and because and I had acquired a tight image by not playing many hands, and because that particular hand type plays well shorthanded, and also perhaps because I have a sense of humor, I ventured to reraise before the flop, hoping to narrow the action.

Lo and behold, the result was three-way action. Guess who? The same three players who had played the above hands.

And when my reraise got back to my right-hand opponent, he quickly capped it saying, "See, just like I said. All you have to do is raise."

For those of you who righteously scoff at my reraise on 6 5 5 3, how would you like my position if I told you that my right-hand opponent, not unexpectedly, held a K Q J 10. He shouldn't be raising before the flop and narrowing the action with a high hand that needs company to be profitable. My other opponent held pocket aces with a jack and 10. I had the only low!

With my opponents holding six high cards, I rate to make a low about 58% of the time (according to Caro's Poker Probe). And even against those two formidable high holdings, I win high, the equivalent to the whole pot, about 43% of the time! All in all, I clearly had the best expectation of winning—almost 60% of the time and getting 2 to 1 odds on my money.

In the real life hand, I won only half (low) of that pot, although I had high won until the last card. When my right-hand opponent saw my hand, I received yet another lecture on how could I possibly reraise with such a bad hand. He might catch on eventually.

## BREAD-AND-BUTTER HANDS

When asked what the most typical "bread-and-butter" hand is at Omaha high-low, most players guess an A 2 and probably think of the times that the A 2 wins the low half of a pot. But did you know that when you hold a typical A 2-nothing special hand (for example, A 2 8 J), you hit a playable low flop, with two or three low cards and no ace or deuce bust, only about one-third of the time? More specifically, you hit about 6.5% of the time for the three different low cards and about 28% of the time for two low cards with no ace or deuce.

**160**

Of the third of the time that you get a good low flop, you end up with a nut low with no ace or deuce bust only about 15% of the time! I ran a simulation to see what the actual numbers are. Of the 6.5% three low-card flops, you subsequently bust (get ace or deuce) about 1.65% of the time. Of the 20% two low-card flops, you hit a low on the fourth card 9.5% of the time, but of those, you bust on fifth 1.3% of the time. You make your nut low on the last card about 5.1% of the time. Thus, when you play an A 2 and get a good flop, you end up with the nut low only about 15% of the time—and not quartered only about 10% of the time in a ten-handed game—assuming all A 2 hands play.

Nevertheless, since an A 2 makes a nut low with almost one-fifth of all hands, including backdoor, the A 2 is still the most valuable single holding at loose Omaha high-low, except perhaps pocket aces *if* you can play them shorthanded—and in some games you can by raising before the flop.

A 3 and 2 3 each make a nut low slightly less than 10% of the time; A 4 and 2 4 each make a nut low less than 5% of the time. There is also value when you pursue an A 2 unsuccessfully (that keeps you in the pot) and a plan B win materializes from your other cards.

Although in a very loose game, more than half of your winnings comes from prime low starting hands such as A 2, A 3, and perhaps some 2 3 and A 4, it has long been my opinion that in not-so-loose to tightish games, an aggressive good player's main source of winnings is the little back-in opportunistic hands which are often high-only.

While thinking about a typical example hand, I was playing $4/$8 Omaha high-low on the Internet. I crawled in sixth position with the A♠ J♠ 8♥ 3♣. It was five-way action, and the flop came J♣ 9♣ 4♠. There were three checks around to me, so I made the obvious bet.

There was some chance that the other four players would fold, and there was some chance that my pair of jacks was currently the best hand. And I certainly do not want to give anyone with an A 2 a free card—I want to make him fold or pay.

Obviously you would prefer to make this bet after a **rainbow** flop, one of three different suits, since you might well get one or more callers with two clubs. And the one time in three when another club hits the board on either of the last two cards, you should seriously reconsider your prospects in this hand. If you get only one caller, you will probably bet after any non-club fourth card. One opponent will fold enough times to make that bet pay for itself in the long run.

Note that this hand had both low and nut-flush backdoor potential. The existence of any secondary prospects, which require both fourth and fifth cards to complete, adds a few percentages to your likelihood of winning. Backdoor lows, flushes, and straights make a big difference when they hit.

Did I say secondary? It was three-way action, and as the 7♠ turned, I found myself looking at a real nut-flush draw and a second-nut low draw (and also a gut shot 10 for a bad straight). It went two checks to me. If I had had just the draws, I might welcome the free card. But, since I also had the jack (top pair with ace kicker), I felt I had to bet to see if either opponent would be nice enough to fold. If a check-raise was lurking (probably on the 10 8 which I was supposed to have), well, then I would just have to draw a spade or a low.

Unfortunately, they both called. Then the internet went into one of those fifteen-second little pauses as we awaited the last card; obviously I was rooting for the 2♠. But the last card was the nasty-looking 7♥. No flush, no low, no straight.

It went bet, fold to me. I don't usually play hero and try to catch bluffs; but this particular player had tried bluffing several times in the past hour. So I paid him off, and, lo and behold, he was bluffing with his disappointed straight-flush draw (K♣ 10♣).

We all have seen hundreds of ways to back into these sometimes annoying and frustrating little pots which are often up for grabs. So, why not try to grab a few? How often do these little pots occur? It all depends on what you call little and on what the rest of the table is doing. My estimate is that between 30% and 60% of all pots—depending on the looseness of the game—are in this opportunistic or chaotic category. For me, these little opportunistic hands are the real bread-and-butter hands in most Omaha high-low games, in all except the loosest games.

## AN OFFBEAT HAND

After an untimely exit from a no-limit hold 'em tournament, you are seeking consolation and further enlightenment in a $5/$10 Omaha high-low game with a kill. You're in late position, and with five players already in the pot, you pick up K♥ 4♥ 5♣ 2♠. Is this a good call at loose Omaha high-low?

Although I suspected that this hand might be even less than marginal in a good game, I was feeling adventurous, and I strongly suspected that this hand was probably better than the hands some of the callers were playing. So I called. Several days later I ran this hand on Mike Caro's Poker Probe against five other random players. I won about 21% of the time, which tends to indicate that the hand is somewhat better than marginal.

I was immediately sorry I had played, as the button raised before the flop and the player in second seat reraised. Although I realized that it would probably get capped out as the button raiser would probably make the third raise—there was the usual three-raise limit in effect, I would not confess error, if indeed I had erred by calling initially. So I put my $10 in, and, sure enough, the button reraised, and it cost me yet another $5.

So there we all were, seven-way action and $140 in the pot. The first card of the flop was an unexpected ace, of which there probably were very few left in the deck, but the next two cards were a 6 and a queen. All were different suits.

Apparently, no one really liked the flop, because it was checked around to me. Although I did not have much, I suspected that if I bet, the button in back of me might raise, thereby pressuring the other five callers.

Sure enough, the button raised my bet, and three of the callers folded. Obviously I only called, since all I had was potential. If you could call for any card to come on the turn, with this hand and flop, what card would you ask for?

The 3♥ hit the turn and gave me an unbreakable low—I would have the nut low whatever the last card was—and the nut flush draw. By the way, if you ever play a hand like this, I can't promise that you will catch an ace and a 3 in the flop. Please remember that I prefaced this section by expressing doubt about playing this sort of hand.

Okay. Now for your final poker challenge. The first two players checked around to me. What should I do? Bet? Do you understand the problem here?

If I bet, it might get called by the button, and I probably would get one or two callers. If the button raises, I might even find myself heads up with him.

But if I check (!), there is about a 2 or 3 to 1 chance that the button will bet and get the same one or two callers. Then my check-raise would probably get considerably more money into the pot, and I might even get a chance to cap it. The times that the button checks are easily more than offset by the potential gain of the check-raise. So I checked, he bet, both called, I raised, and all three called. Okay—but it could have been better!

A happy ending? You bet! Although a heart would have given me three-quarters of this giant pot, a 4 on the river gave me the whole thing! The button, who had started with an ABD hand (A 2 4), succumbed to my 2 5, as did the trip queens.

Yes, I was very lucky. But when you play three prime (ace through 5) low cards, there are lots of ways to get lucky.

## THE UGLY AND THE BAD
You're playing in an Omaha high-low tournament, and you have average chips going into level three—50/100. On your big blind you pick up an ugly 10♠ 2♠ 4♣ 2♣. Opponent one on your left raises before the flop. There is only one caller around to you. Do you defend your blind?

Although you probably would avoid these second-best holdings at loose Omaha high-low with five or more callers, because making your low or flush would too often be second-best, at shorthanded play this ugliness is not so bad. So I defended my blind.

To give you an overview of this situation, opponent one (left) had the A♥ 9♥ and a 6 and a 2; opponent two (right) had the A♣ 5♣ and a 4 and a jack. Running these three hands on Mike Caro's Poker Probe indicates that before the flop, opponent one wins 42% of the time, opponent two wins

27% of the time, and I win 31% of the time—so I probably had my call.

The flop was favorable: J♠ 3♠ 5♥. That gave me a draw for a wheel (ace) or a 6-high straight and a spade flush draw. Everybody seemed to like the flop; there was a bet and a raise to me, which I called. Simulating these hands with this flop on Poker Probe indicates that opponent one now wins only 32% of the time, opponent two (with top two pair) now wins 38% of the time, and I win 30% of the time.

The turn card was the less-than-helpful 3♥, which gave opponent one the big heart flush draw in addition to his nut low draw. So he bet; we both called. This turn card did not change the expectations much. According to Poker Probe, opponent one now wins about 32% of the time, opponent two now wins about 40% of the time, and I win 28% of the time.

I was rooting for the final card to be an ace, a 6, or a spade. But it wasn't. The card that did come up, however, gave me the whole pot (about 1,000 chips; no one bet), which put me in good contention. Quiz question: can you figure out what the fifth card was? Answer given at end of the chapter.

With two tables remaining, the stakes went up to no-limit with the blinds at 200 and 400. After suffering a big loss, I was hurting—I had less than 3,000 chips remaining, and 200 were now in the pot as my big blind.

Two of the eight remaining players limped in for the 200; both of those players were also short-stacked. The little blind called. Based on their previous aggressive performances, I judged that none of the opponents had a good hand. Looking at an 8 5 suited, an ace, and a queen, I attempted to pick up the 800 in the pot by moving all in with my 2,700! The two crawlers folded; the little blind, who had about 5,000 chips, held pocket jacks, a king-suited and a 10. Would you call a 2,700 raise with this hand with 3,500 total in pot?

"I can't let you steal it," he said and called. We faced our hands. Although some might find his high hand attractive, his was actually a bad call, as his hand rated to win less than 30% of the time against a typical raise such as ace and several low cards. Although his hand would be a good hand at high Omaha, at Omaha high-low, a high-only hand has a sound positive expectation only when there are numerous callers and a high flop.

The actual result was that his jacks lost high when I made two pair. I also made an emergency low, which would have saved me half the pot, even if he had won high. The bottom line is that he should have found a greener pasture in which to invest over half of his chips.

## TWO FINAL TABLE HANDS

When the fortunate nine to eleven players reassemble to begin play at the final table of a big poker tournament, for at least the first few hands, there seems to be an almost pious atmosphere at the table. Many players, perhaps feeling somewhat reborn, start anew with resolution to play their best game. And generally, most players tend to start off playing rather tight.

Not for long, though. When the final table gets down to four or five players, everything changes dramatically. Off with the gloves. Especially at no limit tournaments, stacks fly. It seems that many aggressive players think that the solution to most betting-situation problems is to bet your stack. Betting your stack is certainly the ultimate weapon. But the more often you bet your stack, the more likely you are to lose it.

At a recent hold 'em ShootOut Tournament, I was playing head-to-head against a very aggressive player who went all-in before the flop about seven times during our forty-minute-long battle. I folded the first six times, but on his last all-in effort I held pocket kings—which held up. During this match, I went all-in only twice—once before the flop with pocket 10s, at which point he folded, and once on one of the following two action hands.

I started slightly ahead in chips but the large blind and ante structure led to hot competition in which the lead alternated almost every hand. With about 150 chips in play and blinds at 2 and 4 plus one chip ante, on most hands there would be a ten to twenty chip raise before the flop, usually folded. On one key hand I picked up the jack and 10 of clubs. He acted first and made it ten to go (six to me if I called). Judging from his previous raises, he probably had at least one high card or two medium cards, but, as always, there was the remote chance that he was baiting with a big hand—such as pocket aces or kings. At this point he had gone all in before the flop only once.

If I called with my jack-ten suited, on most flops he would probably lead bet ten chips or more—we each started the hand with about seventy chips. I had noted that earlier he had displayed great tenacity calling reraises on several hands. Thus, if I made a big bet against him, the combined chances of his folding plus my hitting would be a bit less than usual. Regarding my general all-in prospects, I judged that if there was as much as a one in four chance that he would call and win, then that risk would not be worth taking. And that probably applied to this hand.

So, instead of merely calling, I decided to play my position and attempt to grab the initiative by making a measured raise. I raised a mere "mind-game" ten. Based on his play, I judged that he was at least a good player and that he would consider that I might be baiting him with a big pair. He thought briefly and called.

The flop came K♠ 10♥ 7♣. Hitting the pair of 10s was good, but the presence of the king was scary. He checked to me. Note well the dualities which apply in these situations. He would be most likely to bet a medium-to-bad hand. He would probably check any good hand, and most bad hands. Because I had hit the second high pair on the flop, checking this hand clearly would be unsound. What bet would give me the best all around chances? There were now forty-two chips (two antes) in the pot, and we each had fifty-odd chips left. What would you do in this tough situation?

If I went all in he would probably call only with kings or better. Based on his earlier folding practices and his actions this hand, I estimated that he would have kings or better roughly 20-30% of the time—roughly one out of four times. Remember how I said that I was unwilling to risk losing roughly one out of four times at this point?

I considered for a moment. Since my small reraise before the flop might have been based on pocket aces or kings, or even ace-king, what would I now bet if I had hit three kings? I certainly would bet a small amount to tempt him to call; but I would bet enough to give him bad odds on an inside straight draw. I bet a mere fifteen. I watched him very closely, because there was some chance that he would push his stack.

He thought about it and folded. In retrospect, it might have been better for me to have bet my stack instead of the cute fifteen, because if he had raised all in, I would have had a big problem. Comments welcome.

The next hand I'll describe was my reactionary hand for the match. From the standpoint of value, it was clearly unsound.

I had been ahead in chips about 2 to 1. Then, on my next four big blinds, when I was acting last, my opponent went all in before the flop three times out of the four, because he was behind. I had nothing resembling a call. On one of his big blind hands that I had raised a dime before the flop, he reraised all-in and caught me with a K 9 offsuit. Again I folded, he probably had me beat going in. He had fought his way back and at that time had a slight lead in chips.

The blinds and antes went up to 10 and 6 (8 and 4 plus 2 ante). I was acting first, and I picked up an A 7. At head-to-head I normally would make a small raise of perhaps 10 to 20. But I had a feeling that he would press his luck and reraise all in. If that happened, I might want to call, but I certainly would not like it. He certainly was getting the best of it, and I did not like my negative momentum. Would you simply make the normal raise here?

I reacted and decided to step out. I pushed in my stack. Fight fire with fire! Let him decide whether I had something or not. If he called, my ace should give me some play. He mulled it over for some time. Although he might have been acting, it did seem as if he actually had a problem. But he finally folded. He might have folded a decent hand. If I had bet a small amount he might well have reraised all in, based on the vigorish of my folding. So I gained a slight lead in chips. But I also regained the momentum. On the next hand he crashed into my pocket kings. Strange how luck often follows the momentum at no limit.

*Answer to Quiz Question: The final board card was a third 3! Hence my tiny full house won the whole pot because there was no low.*

# 8 LET'S PLAY AROUND

## CAPPELLETTI IN ATLANTIC CITY

Although I have often expressed my opinion that there is considerably more skill in straight high Omaha, especially pot limit, than in Omaha high-low, mostly because the bi-directionality makes judgment less accurate, there are certainly many hands at Omaha high-low on which guessing the opponents' holdings enables you to optimize your results.

You're on the button in a loose $5/$10 Omaha high-low game. You pick up A♥ 4♥, and a deuce and a jack. Four players crawl in to you, and, of course, you raise. Any A 2 is an adequate raise in a well-attended pot, but this hand also has the very significant 4 and nut-flush holding. The little blind folds, but all others call, which makes six-way action.

The flop comes A♦ J♦ 9♥. You would have preferred low cards, especially with a 3 and some hearts, but at least you have top two pair. It gets checked around to the player in front of you, who bets. Since there already is a good starting pot, you raise to put pressure on the straight draws, low flush draws, and the 2 3s. You get one caller, three opponents fold, and the bettor just calls. The bettor's mere calling is a good sign, because he probably would have bent it back with trip aces, or perhaps with lower trips. You had noted on earlier hands that this bettor had eagerly bet two pair and flush draws.

The three of spades turns, giving you the nut low draw. The lead bettor bets again in front of you. Do you want the caller in or should you try to raise him out? What is the bettor betting on? If he has his bet, for instance, trip 9s or jacks, there is no advantage in my increasing my draw investment. But if he is pushing (and we know he likes to bet) something like aces over 9s and perhaps a low draw, it would be best to get a possible flush or straight draw out of the running. Then again, now that you have the nut low draw, it might be good to have another potential caller if you hit one of the sixteen 5s through 8s, especially the 5s. But if one of the six 4s or deuces hits, you would rather have the caller out, although the bettor might have a low.

All-in-all, since you might be drawing, and the caller just might have trips, you should probably just call. I did. The river card was a classic "good news-bad news" card: the 8♦. I had just made the nut low, but now there was not only a likely flush, but also a possible straight Q 10 or 10 7.

Again, the lead bettor bet out. It looked like he had been pushing a flush draw and perhaps had hit a low. Now, what did the caller have? My first inclination was simply to call and get him in for one more bet. But if he had a flush draw and/or a low, he might stick around for a raise. I might pressure him out by raising, also fearing reraises, or I might be getting quartered.

Generally, if you have any reasonable chances of winning the whole pot, it is best to raise out a caller who might inch you out of one direction. But at the table at that time, it looked very unlikely that I had the bettor beat for high *and* that the caller had me beat with a high holding that might fold a raise. So I just called. And the caller called—as expected.

Lo and behold, the bettor was pushing jacks and 9s and a bad low. And the caller had made trip 3s on the turn! So if I had raised, I probably would have won the whole pot!

Should I have raised? While playing along, did you? In retrospect, since the bettor was suspected to be a questionable, or perhaps semi-random player, it probably would have been slightly better to raise.

# CAPPELLETTI IN BILOXI

While playing in a loose and lively $4/$8 Omaha high-low game with a half kill at the Biloxi Grand, I called in late position with A J 10 4, ace was suited. It was seven-way action, and the flop came 9 8 3, which gave me the second-nut low draw (a 7, 6 or 5 would give me second-nut low; but a 2 would give me the nut low) and a two-way straight draw.

Amazingly, all six players in front of me checked. If, after the flop, your main prospect is a second-nut low draw, there are various conflicting considerations in deciding whether to bet or to check. Perhaps the best argument for checking is if a known very tight player, one who often has an A 2, has called to see the flop. Perhaps the best argument for betting is simply that someone should bet to narrow the action or build the pot since there were many callers before the flop, and most rate to have worse prospects than you.

Note that mathematically, in a ten-handed game, there will be an A 2 out against you about half the time, assuming any A 2 would see the flop. Thus in a well-attended pot, your low potential is adequate, break-even or better, to justify making the marginal bet. And, if anyone folds, your high potential usually increases; hence your overall expected return should increase by more than the amount of the bet. In loose Omaha high-low, when many players call with inadequate hands, most dubious situations should be resolved in favor of getting more money into the pot and not giving free cards.

In addition, it is advantageous both strategically and tactically to gain the initiative by betting. Unlike in tight hold 'em, in Omaha you make more money by getting more callers, so there is a tangible intrinsic value simply in being the bettor.

On the given hand, since I also had good high potential (the two-way straight draw), betting for value seemed correct. I was reaching for my chips to bet, when the player in front of me, who had seemed like he was about to check, suddenly decided to bet. Now things have changed. Should I call or raise?

If I had had a slightly worse hand in this situation, with many before-the-flop callers checking around, such as a gut straight draw, instead of the two-way, or a 3 4, third-nut low instead of second-nut low, I would normally make the promo raise! If a bad-hand with two-way potential is good enough to call, then it is probably right to raise if a raise rates to narrow the field substantially.

In the given situation, though, my hand was good enough simply to call and pull, reduce investment and increase payoff odds. Note that the main value of a tactical raise here would be that it might pressure out another A 4, if there was one in back of me.

So I merely called as did three others. It was five-way action, and the turn card was the J♦, which made a straight possible. It went check around to me. Since I now had some semblance of a made high hand—a pair of jacks with ace-high—it was probably right to bet to see if anyone would fold, and to take the initiative. Two players folded. Note how the "bird-in-hand" card completely changed my strategy from pull to push.

It was three-way action, and the river card was a 4, which counterfeited my low chances but improved my high, which was a two pair. It went check around to me, so I checked. Not surprisingly, I had the best high. But neither opponent had a low, so I was forced to take the whole pot! If I hadn't bet the turn, probably one of the two opponents that folded would have had a bad low. All-in-all, it was a fairly nice pot to win considering that I did not particularly like either of the last two cards. A surprisingly large portion of your Omaha high-low winnings comes from opportunistic/lucky, not-so-good hands.

Just before the Omaha high-low tournament started, there was jackpot magic in the air. On blind, I flopped a nut low with my 2 3. Then I sat back, fearing being quartered, and watched as two high hands capped it out on the turn and river, with aces-full versus four queens! Somebody cried out, "Jackpot," but the Omaha bad-beat jackpot required four-of-a-kind or better. However, barely two minutes later, at the next table where I had played hold 'em before getting a high-low seat, someone hit a $14,000 jackpot! Close, but no cigar.

## CAPPELLETTI IN TUNICA

As I drove into Tunica County, I first passed the Grand Casino, but then U-turned back to check it out. The Grand has a large poker room, and on that Monday afternoon it had a $5/$10 Omaha high-low with a full kill going, in addition to $10/$20 hold 'em and several $4/$8 hold 'em tables. The bad beat hold 'em jackpot (quads losing) was about $75,000, which undoubtedly accounted for some of the hold 'em action.

The Grand also has several well-attended weekly poker tournaments (five or six tables of hold 'em or Omaha high-low) with a $5 entry fee, $15 rebuys, and "an offer you can't refuse" add-on at $25 dollars. I played in their Tuesday noontime hold 'em tournament, and got knocked out just prior to the final table.

Picture this scenario, a player is playing nine-handed pot limit high Omaha, with a $500 buy in. On a $25 big blind, he holds 8 7 7 3 rainbow, and four players call including the little blind. He's played in this game for about an hour, and noticed that there had been a raise before the flop on about one-third of the hands. The flop comes K♥ 7♥ 4♣. His $600+ is the second smallest stack since I bought in small for $500; several seasoned and perhaps good players have 5,000 plus in chips and $100 bills in front of them. The little blind leads with $100. Should he fold, call, or raise?

I know that many players tend to jump in head-first every time they flop a set as I did on this hand. Perhaps the best answer to the question is that it all depends on how solid or conservative the lead better is. If he would tend to have a set of kings (trips) about half of the time, clearly the player should fold, since he only has $25 in the pot.

Note that, looking at his four cards and the three flop cards, if one dealt out eight four-card hands, one of the eight hands would contain two or three kings about 14% of the time. One would win a head-to-head confrontation against pocket kings less than one-fifth of the time.

During the previous hour, I had been uninvolved in all but one hand on which two players dropped my pot raise after the flop. Although I am not sure the pot-raise is always correct in this situation, in this instance I felt that I should step out and risk my $600 to gain the $200, or whatever the traffic had put in. The two other opponents folded my pot raise, but the little blind reraised, and I put my last $200+ all in.

I wasn't sure that I liked the king on the turn card as it gave him trip kings, but it was actually fortuitous for me, since he flushed on the last card. My little boat won the $1,300+ pot. Several rounds later, holding a nut flush, I raised a $400 bet to $1,200, but everyone folded.

There's a theory that when you play pot- or no-limit poker, it is best to have the most money on the table or just a minimum buy-in. In no-limit Omaha, when you flop or turn the nuts, it is quite advantageous to get all your money into the pot. You thus deprive any drawer of a subsequent bet if he hits and beats you (or bluffs). If you start "small" and increase your minimum buy-in to four or five times its original size, it is sometimes best to harvest your win and come back small on a later occasion. For example, if you start at $500, build it up to $2,000, and then take on players holding over $10,000, it is rather likely that you will lose a hand and go broke before conquering the big stacks.

After a wonderful supper, I bought in again for the minimum $500, which quickly grew to about $700. Several rounds later, I saw the flop with A♥ 4♥ Q♦ 6♦. The flop came Q♥ 7♥ 3♣. I called the usual $100 after-the-flop bet, as did my left hand opponent—three way action. Note that if a 5 came on fourth street, which would give me a nut straight, I'd be more likely to get paid off than if the turn card were a heart. Lucky me—the 5♣ turned! This was the set up that I had been waiting for.

The lead bettor bet a sneaky $100; I had just enough to raise the pot and go all-in—about $600. The left-hand opponent made it $1,500! The lead bettor dropped—perfect! Even if the left-hand opponent also had a 6 4, I still had the extra nut-heart draw.

We tabled our cards; he had been waiting with trip queens (top set). But he had waited too long, because now I was more than a 3-1 favorite (31-9). But another 5 paired the board on the river, and his full house won. Unlucky.

Enough of this big money excitement. Still up a grand from my earlier effort, I quit and retired to the relative safety of limit Omaha high-low.

## CAPPELLETTI IN COSTA RICA

While I was playing in a rather loose $20/$40 Omaha high-low game at the Casino Europa in San Jose, Costa Rica, one of the Californian visitors asked me if I would object to having a kibitzer. I certainly didn't object, but I warned him that he might not see much action, since I fold a large number of hands.

True to my word, I folded the next five hands before the flop. On my big blind, though, I picked up the 5♥ 4♥, along with an ace and a 3. A player who usually played only good starting hands raised in second seat, and it was folded around to me—a rare occurrence in that game.

So I defended my blind. As the dealer centered the chips and prepared to flop, the kibitzer whispered in my ear, "Why didn't you reraise?"

I whispered back to him that I didn't reraise because I rated to be an underdog.

He said, "Oh I can't believe that!"

I said, "Believe it!"

The simple truth of the matter is that all wonderful low hands (such as A 2 3 4) are not that good at head-to-head. So whenever a deal seems to be shaping up to a head-to-head dogfight, it is obviously important to know where you stand with four low cards.

Note that the hand A 3 4 5 with the 5 4 suited does win about 54.5% of the time against a random hand. Against an ace and three random cards, though, that hand wins only about 46% of the time since a before-the-flop raiser often has an ace. And against an A 2 and two random cards or two aces and two random cards, the A 3 4 5 wins slightly less than 42% of the time. Thus, I rated to be a slight underdog.

The flop came J♦ 8♦ and a 3. I checked; my opponent bet $20; I called. Note that even the nut low draw is not a winning hand with little high potential, and I had second-nut low draw.

The turn card was the 5♠. He bet the $40. Now I had both the second-nut low and two pair. That's more than enough to call with but no reason to get excited. I could easily be beat both ways as before-the-flop raisers often have A 2, or I could get quartered.

The last card was the 6♣. It didn't help me, but it might have helped my opponent because he might have made a straight or second pair. He bet the $40. Obviously I had to call, but I wouldn't have been surprised to lose both ways, for example, if he held an A 2 4. I certainly didn't consider raising.

Then my opponent threw his hand down on the table in disgust. He had a king, queen, and the 10♦ 9♦, a straight flush draw on the flop. But he had hit nothing. I was actually rather surprised to scoop the pot.

Note that my opponent's before-the-flop raise on a straight high hand is unwise at Omaha high-low. High hands are mainly playable with a high flop, which occurs about one time in four and with a large number of before-the-flop callers, most of whom will have mainly low cards. A before-the flop raise tends to decrease the number of callers, which might make the payoff of the pots you win inadequate to offset the much larger number of pots that you lose.

As they were dealing the next hand, my kibitzer said, "How come you didn't raise him at the end?"

I replied, "I was much closer to folding than raising."

He shook his head in total disbelief.

He clearly did not understand that with many opponents it would be quite likely for him to have held an A 2 for his early seat raise, especially if he was one of the players that raise before the flop only with an A 2 or pocket aces. Perhaps the main reason why loose Omaha high-low allows the expert players to average over two-and-a-half big bets per hour, whereas expert hold 'em players usually average about one-and-a-half big bets per hour is that most average or worse Omaha players have little or no knowledge of many of these basic concepts of Omaha.

## TALES FROM THE CONNECTICUT WOODS

While driving from Virginia to Rhode Island, on Interstate 95, I stopped in Foxwoods. And I "just happened" to be in time for the hold 'em tournament.

In the hold 'em tournament, I cleverly avoided the final table by investing too many chips in pocket aces. This mistake enabled me to discover a little piece of heaven there in the backwoods of Connecticut—namely a $5/$10 Omaha high-low game with a **kill,** when someone scoops a $100+ pot, he blinds $10 in the next hand, which is played at double stakes—$10/$20. There were very few pots with fewer than six callers! And several of the players were novices, with stacks of green chips from other endeavors.

On another occasion, in about three hours, I managed to complete row three of my triangular chip pyramid and I was working on row four. The following two hands might communicate some of the flavor of this game.

In late seat with many callers, I raised before the flop with an A 2 4 6. K 7 5 flopped. There was a bet and a call to me. I made the mandatory raise with A 2 4, to pressure an A 3 or 2 3, the hands that would beat me for low if an ace or deuce turned, and I was also happy to raise because I had good two-way prospects. The button in back of me reraised and announced, "I'm reraising with top-two," it had become fashionable and humorous among several of the other players to announce what they held. And someone else capped the five-way action!

A second 5 turned. It was checked around to me, so I bet my high-percentage tickets, allowing no free rides. The "top two" player in back of me raised; two of the remaining three players called, as did I. Was the last card a storybook 8 or 3? No—the last card was a miserable third 5! No low. No nothing!

But the two players on my right also looked very disappointed at the last card. If my left-hand opponent really did have "top two" pair (and he had told the truth several times earlier), he might not have the fourth 5. So I decided to bet and hope. I have seen some amazing things happen when low does not make it and no one has a good high.

And something amazing did happen! When the "top two" player to my left called, everyone assumed he had a pocket pair or even the fourth 5. The other two players folded dejectedly. I showed my hand and joked, "Nut low," but there was no low.

He spread his hand and said, "I have 5s full of kings and 7s."

We were both wrong! He showed a K Q 10 7! The dealer had to explain that he had no full house, and my ace with the three 5s beat his two pair. One player who folded said he could have beat my ace-nothing, but he might not have called. Thus I scooped close to $300 with my ace-high!

My next tale is somewhat more of a routine. On the button with seven callers in front of me, I chose to raise before the flop with 5 4 3 2 double-suited, almost any good button hand can raise profitably on sheer numbers. My raise was instantly justified when an ace flopped, and it was accompanied by a 7 and a queen. Someone bet, two players called, someone raised, and someone called. I made it three bets, and the four remaining players all called. A 4 hit the turn. Now that I actually had something—the nut low (2 3) with extension card (5)—I raised and reraised. Four players each put in $40. I was rooting for a 2, 3 or 5.

Then came the storybook ending—a 3, which neatly counterfeited the other 2 3 and gave me a wheel to scoop the pot and add three more stacks of chips to my pyramid.

## AT FOXWOODS

I was playing $10/$20 Omaha high-low at Foxwoods which was actually a "kill" pot in a $5/$10 game, and I was in the second seat. I picked up the K♠ J♠, a queen, and a 10.

The first person to act folded, and I simply called. Although I might well raise with this hand at Omaha straight high, it would be foolish to raise with this hand at high-low, since all one-way high hands need lots of company seeing the flop to be profitable. For example, if I raised and only the killer, who has already posted $10, called with a completely random hand, he would be a favorite to beat me. On Mike Caro's Poker Probe, my hand rates to win only about 45% of the time versus a random hand and less than 40% of the time against an ace.

Yet, in general, playing any straight high hand against three or more opponents is quite profitable. You usually continue to play only after a high flop, and that occurs about one-fourth of the time. And we note that those starting pots have been nicely enlarged by the low hands, who often continue to fish in.

It was four-way action, and I got a high flop—Q♣ 9♣ 2♠. The big blind checked, and I made the obvious bet. At that point, I had a reasonable high hand (top pair and 13-card straight draw) and it was imperative to pressure the two-card low draws. Given my hand, the last two cards will make a low on the board almost one-third of the time. The two callers both folded and gave up on their lows. But the big blind check-raised! What should I do now?

What kind of hand might he have to have check-raised? The best possible hand—an already made hand—would be pocket queens or perhaps pocket 9s. He might have merely a queen and a 9, making "top two." But would he really check the flop with these holdings and risk giving the lows a free card? And since all of those mentioned hands were hidden, wouldn't it be far more profitable in the long run simply to bet, since high flops are often checked out in weak games?

So, I asked myself, what do I know about this player? Is he a solid type? Does he frequently check-raise? Does he bet the flop a lot? Is he an imaginative player?

But wait! The most important question here is this one: how well does this player know the game? Is he a very good high Omaha player? If he's a good high Omaha player and knows that check-raising is a high-percentage move in this situation, he might be reraising on almost anything!

Look at this situation from my perspective. Assuming I call his check-raise, if the turn card pairs the board or is a third club, and he bets out, I would have to fold, since I am probably drawing dead.

Now consider the odds from his perspective. If he understands that most (good) aggressive players would bet in late seat with most high hands, then I rate to have one of four types of hands:

• **A pair type hand**—with as much as trips or two pairs and as little as one pair
• **A flush draw**—in this case that's two clubs, preferably with ace or king
• **A straight draw**—with eight or more hits, which is what I actually had
• **A lesser hand**—with none of the above, perhaps some low-percentage draws

Note that the likelihood of each of the four varies from roughly "equally likely" to "highly weighted towards the first two or three"—depending on the propensities of the particular opponent. For example, an aggressive yet fairly tight player such as myself might have the fourth type less than 10% of the time and each of the first three types about 30% of the time. Thus, if the fourth card pairs the board about one-fifth of the time, he could expect me to fold his bet over two-thirds of the time, out of dead fear—fear of drawing dead. If a club hit the board, which will happen slightly more than one-fifth of the time, I would likely fold his bet more than half of the time. Note also that the only bricks, which are non-scary cards—about one third of the cards, on fourth street would be low cards, which might then give him an emergency low draw—in case I actually had a high.

Thus, when all of those equities are added to whatever actual prospects he had, his reraise becomes a high-percentage move indeed—unless I reraise!

This particular player not only seemed to know what he was doing, but I noticed that he had been watching me and my play rather intently. Furthermore, I got the distinct feeling that he had been patiently waiting for the right moment to make a move. And, being in the big blind, he was slightly less likely to hold a big hand, since he had been forced to play.

Okay—time for us to play. Since I was at least going to call, might it not be better to reraise? Why? To check out whether he calls or reraises? Is this beginning to sound like hold 'em? My reraise might scare off a bluff that I might mistakenly fold if I do not reraise and do not like the fourth card, and he makes the likely bet. At the very minimum, since I go last, I rate to get a half-price fifth card! Even if he likes the fourth card, he might check, hoping to raise. Weigh those reasons against the advantage of having him in the pot if I turn good. Clearly the winning-the-pot reasons take precedence over making the pot larger.

So I decided to reraise. Lo and behold, he folded! Obviously, I was very fortunate that he didn't have a real hand. But note that if he had called or reraised and a pair or flush hit the board, I would have had an easy fold.

During the past six months, I have made this speculative reraise after an early check-raise several times, and I've gotten mixed results. The good news was that in every case, the issue (whether the check-raiser really had a hand or was willing to keep pushing a bluff) was resolved quickly and did not go to the river. Since I won several of these efforts, I clearly came out ahead money-wise. Nonetheless, I will emphasize that this move would be much less effective against a solid player—he would almost always have his check-raise.

## INSURANCE IN HARTFORD

Hartford is often referred to as the "insurance capital," because it's home office of many old-line, large insurance companies. While there, I was fortunate enough to hold a rare Omaha perfect "insurance hand," which is unbeatable after the flop.

A perfect low **insurance hand** is one on which you hold four prime low cards and the fifth prime low card hits the flop with two other low cards. On these rare hands, you can set your mind at ease, since you cannot be double-counterfeited. And unlike many other low-hand situations in Omaha high-low, these hands are strictly pull hands, since you do not want to narrow the field.

I was playing in a lively Omaha high-low $5/$10 with a kill, and I was in next-to-last position. I picked up an A 2 4 5. With six players in the pot, I made the obvious raise before the flop. It was then seven-way action, and I got a great low flop: 3 7 8. Note that not only did I have the nut low, but I would continue to have a nut low no matter what hit the board on the last two cards. That's a truly unbreakable low.

With hands like this one, your prime strategy should be to keep players in and to build the pot. The first player bet, and there were four callers around to me. Obviously, I raised. There was a call and a reraise (by an A 2, I found out later). Since it seemed like everyone was going to call, I capped it. Everyone called. If I had thought that reraising would have made anyone fold, I wouldn't have reraised.

It was now five-way action, and an ace hit the table, bringing grief to the other A 2. I still had the nut low with the 2 4, and now I also had aces for high.

The first player (with trips) led the betting again. Everyone called around to me; I raised. Everyone called except the holder of the A 2; he finally folded, which he should have done on the previous bet. Then the player on my right reraised (with his 2 4, as I later learned) into the four-way action. A reraise by me might make one—or even two—players fold. Should I reraise?

Yes! Things had changed a bit. Now I had a clear reraise to exert pressure on the highs and perhaps make some weakish high holdings fold, which would thus promote the high chances of my aces. So I reraised—but they all called anyway.

It was now four-way action, and the river card was a 4! This busted the other 2 4, but I still had the nut low with my 2 5, which also now made a wheel. That gave me good chances for high also. At this point, only a 5 6, which would make an 8-high straight, could beat me for high.

It went check around to me. I suspected that I had a big scoop coming. I bet, and the trip 7s and busted 2 4 both called. Needless to say, the next hand was a kill pot. Go East, young man?

Note that this was one hand where, after the flop, I did not have to fear the fickle finger of Omaha on the turn and the river. And notice how fate neatly picked off my first two nut lows. Fortunately, I had the extra coverage—call it "whole life protection" on this hand, since I was fully insured against being outdrawn.

Hands like this, on which you have both insurance cards after the flop, are extremely rare. They are somewhat similar to hands on which you have both (straight) "extension cards" in high Omaha. Most often, these insurance hands occur after the fourth card—you might have the nut low, and you also hold the next lowest "insurance card," which would make a nut low if one of your nut low cards is counterfeited on the last card. Having the insurance card usually affects your odds and strategy and often justifies aggressive, rather than the usual conservative, low play.

## CAPPELLETTI IN LONDON

After six wonderful hours in the British Museum and a nice Indian supper with my family, I taxied over to the Victoria Club Casino. Since I already was a member, I did not have to wait forty-eight hours to play, as required by British law, if you are planning to visit London, you should take steps to join in advance.

When I had last been at the Vic, about seven years earlier, pot-limit hold 'em had been the rage. But on this Friday evening, there appeared to be even more Omaha high pot-limit tables going than hold 'em tables. I played some relatively loose pot-limit hold 'em while waiting. Then I took a seat at an even looser 500-pound buy-in Omaha table with two 10-pound blinds.

One of the first hands with which I voluntarily called was a K Q 10 9 wrap. I was fourth to act of six players who had called to see the flop. The flop hit with Q 10 4 (two spades), which gave me top two pair. It was checked around to me. I chose to bet 40 pounds. I got three callers, which is typical of this game—two acted after me; one acted before me.

Instead of the usual nasty flush or straight card on the turn, lo and behold, a second queen hit the table! I now had the top full boat—the nuts. The opponent in front of me checked. Would you bet with my hand, or would you trap?

There is an old theory that if you hit the best possible card on the turn, which gives you a very likely winner, you should trap instead of bet. But I have often professed that in Omaha, as in hold 'em, your first and main concern is to protect your lead by betting on the turn. Especially with fragile holdings, which in Omaha most holdings are, it is crucial to push out various hands which might beat you. When there are very few hands that might beat you, it becomes a question of evaluating how much you get for what you are giving. In the above situation, your queens full will remain the nuts with more than two-thirds of the last cards and only an ace, king, jack, or 4 present a possibility of losing.

The only hands that could beat me on the river and would probably fold a big bet on the turn were pocket aces or kings. In a game with nine original opponents, someone will have pocket aces or kings about half the time, and he will probably see the flop. A player who has fished in after the flop with aces or kings might also call a small bet on the turn. If either aces or kings are present, they would hit and beat me only about 1 time in 20. Thus, my odds of losing to aces or kings full, hands which would have folded a big bet, are probably about 1 in 40.

In the above scenario, if you make a large bet on the turn, you rate to get, on average, one caller or fewer. Very rarely will you get action from several players. More often everyone will fold. Once a pair hits the turn, most flush and straight draws give up. And lower full boats are less likely here, since there was no raise (with trips) on the flop. Of course, any full boat behind you will probably bet.

Thus, the main variable in these situations is what kind of players are sitting in back of you. If either player is the aggressive type who might pick up the ball if you check, a check is clearly best. But if both players are passive calling stations, then it would be best to make a medium-sized bet. Note that if you have a tight or tightish image, which most of us do, it is usually better to get a loose player to do the betting for you, since he is more likely to get callers.

All-in-all, against average or unknown players, it is probably best to check. If both subsequent players check, they might well have folded your bet. If it gets checked out, you probably should bet 80 to 100 pounds after the last card (again, that amount depends on who is sitting in back of you and also on what card hits).

If someone bets on the turn, should you raise? I would raise if my left-hand opponent had bet and there were one or two callers trapped in. I would not raise if there were players behind me who might call, or even raise. Probably the best psychological ploy is a slightly indecisive call if that fits in your repertoire.

The bottom line is: when you check after a great fourth card, you might lose a medium-sized bet that you might have extracted from a caller. And, if the last card is very bad, you might lose the pot. But any time someone else bets, you rate to do better than if you had bet. The big gain is when you pull in an aggressive bettor, caller, or bluffer who might have dropped your bet—you gain at least one medium-sized bet. You also might gain from someone who improves on the last card.

I estimate that the end result of checking averages leads to a gain of about two-thirds of the current pot size. Again, subject to your evaluation of the players behind you. With very aggressive opponents, the average gain is clearly more than that. So, in the long run, trapping should gain more than enough to compensate for the one pot in twenty or thirty that you lose, and which might have been saved by betting.

So I checked. The player on my left bet 100 pounds. The other two players folded. I considered raising all-in with the 450 pounds that I had left. But if he was bluffing, betting on the come, or pushing a high pair, any big raise might make him fold, and I'd lose him. I decided simply to call.

Unfortunately, the last card was an ace. I could lose to pocket aces or the case queen with an ace kicker. Should I bet? He looked like he was about to bet. I checked. He mulled a bit, then bet 100 pounds. Did I still have the best hand?

Now that I had drawn him in according to plan, was it time to spring the trap? But there was something about the way he had bet, and I just called. He had the queen with an ace, and he beat me on the last card! Had I made a big bet on the turn, he would have called and then bet me all-in after the last card. So I ended up saving about half of my buy-in. The check turned out better for reasons unforeseen. Funny how quickly things can change in Omaha.

## RETURN TO PARIS

In Paris, poker is played at the fashionable Aviation Club, which is located about two blocks from the Arch of Triumph on the Champs d'Elysee. At about 9:30 each night, the three or four poker games in progress break for about an hour to have a civilized supper at the club's gourmet restaurant.

All games are pot-limit, table stakes, like in England and many other European countries. Most tables had a 1,000F minimum buy-in, about $200.

At the Aviation Club, they play dealer's choice of eight poker games specified on four two-sided tiles stacked that serve as the dealer button. The dealer places his choice on top, thus there is no confusion as to which game is being played. The games specified on the tiles were Texas hold 'em, Omaha (four- or five-card), Omaha high-low, Courceval (Omaha with the first flop card disclosed in advance) and seven-card stud (high or high-low). Courceval seemed to be the most popular game. There were three blinds: 25F, 10F, and 10F.

I played very tight, folding all marginal starting hands. At Courceval, I defended my big blind when I held A♠ 5♠, a 6, and a 2, with the first flop card (showing) the 2♠. Four players each had put 100F into the pot. The rest of the flop was a 3 and a 4, which gave me a nut low straight.

The little blind on my right bet 200F. Because these low straights are so fragile, I raised about 600F, going all in. The bettor called, the other two folded, and my straight held up. Thus, I doubled my buy-in.

Note that one of the most strategic advantages to be gained in pot-limit and in no-limit Omaha is to deprive your drawing opponent of his re-bet if he hits, because either you or he is all-in. Thus, if he hits his draw, he wins merely the current pot, and you avoid one of the most perilous and low-percentage situations in Omaha, when you have the nuts after the fourth card but the last card either flushes or pairs the board, and then your opponent makes a huge bet.

Next we were playing Omaha high-low. Holding A♥ 3♥ with a queen and a jack, I called at 100F to go before the flop.

As in limit Omaha high-low, raising or re-raising on A 3 Q holdings usually accomplishes very little.

With three players, the flop came A J 10 with two diamonds. The first player checked. Since it was unlikely that the last player held a king-queen, I bet 300F with my top two pair, which is the same bet I would make with the king-queen. Note that if I had checked, and the last player had bet the 300F, I would have had to fold. The before-the-flop raiser folded as I had hoped, but the checker called!

The fourth card was a low diamond, and the board now had three diamonds. He checked to me. Fearing that he might have hit a nut flush draw, I checked also. Then I got lucky! The last card was an ace, which gave me the nuts. And he bet 300F at me! I had about 1,500F left. I fingered my chips and raised him 300F. He started making a speech like a character in a French movie. Then he ceremoniously flung his cards into the muck. He was no fool.

I played several more hours the following evening, while my exhausted family slept after a long day of sight-seeing. The first major decision that I had to make was essentially a variation of a classic pot-limit Omaha problem. I was playing Omaha high-low. Holding A♠ 5♠ 4♥ 6♥, I had called 100F before the flop. The flop came Q♠ J♠ 7♦. It was four-way action, and the player in first seat bet 300F. The second player raised 800F. I had about 600F remaining. Would you call all-in or fold?

Normally in pot-limit or no-limit high Omaha, you cannot afford to call a pot-sized bet on a draw hand which hits about one-third of the time. The percentages of a nut flush draw winning, if it hits, are further lessened by the possibility of the board pairing. Had I been playing straight high Omaha, if one of the bettors held trips, which was not likely, I would win the pot less than 30% of the time.

In this situation, though, if I called all-in, I would be sending 600F to win 1,300F, or 300F more if the first bettor called. But because we were playing high-low, with one low card in the flop, there was roughly a 1 in 4 chance of hitting a backdoor low. And, if the first bettor folded and the raise actually had a lesser hand, there was some chance that I might win the pot.

All-in-all, I estimated that there was enough value for the investment. I called all-in. The first bettor re-raised all-in with his top set. But only his first 300F went into my pot. I missed my flush, but two low cards hit the table, and I won half of the 2200F center pot with my backdoor low. All Omaha high-low players must learn to include the possibility of backdoor lows winning in all of their close decisions.

## CAPPELLETTI IN TAMPA

The Semiole Indian Bingo/Casino just off Route 4 outside Tampa has a large poker room. But because of the antiquated Florida state laws, the maximum allowable pot size was $10, therefore the bets were 25¢–50¢! Also, as in the Seminole Casino outside Miami, there were frequent one-table poker tournaments, which were quite popular with the locals—notwithstanding the extremely unfavorable payoffs.

I played in three of the Omaha high-low tournaments, which had ten players each paying a $40 buy-in. After thirty hands, the players with the most chips were awarded 1st, 2nd, and 3rd prize—but they paid out only $290 of the $400 taken in (1st - $150, 2nd - $90, $3rd - $50). The house kept over 27%—that's even worse than race tracks! Although I was fairly lucky in the three tournaments and finished 2nd ($90), 3rd ($50), and 4th, I showed a profit of merely $20.

When I later discussed this with management, I was told that they could not award more than $10 per hand. So why not pay out $300 instead of $290? Their response was that they didn't know. Why not play thirty-two hands and award $320 and keeping a mere 20%? I think the players should organize and picket! Here's another pet peeve of mine: satellite tournaments where management keeps a rip off amount, but probably Florida is the worst.

The tournaments were so loose that 80-90% of players saw each flop and an increase in starting hand selection was in order. I added almost any ace-suited and most A 4 and A 5s, as well as 2 4 5 6, and 2 4 5 7. Notwithstanding this high percentage of participation, the first few hands had no raises before the flop. Then I noticed an interesting phenomenon, which I refer to as "raise with a vengeance." The several times that I chose to raise before the flop, my raises were received almost as acts of open hostility. Several irate prior callers chose to reraise and cap it out before the flop, perhaps to teach me a lesson ("don't throw me into that briar patch").

In a typical Omaha high-low game, scooping a pot with fifty betting units is usually considered a healthy win. In one of the tournament hands, I won over one-hundred betting units, which was only three-fourths of the pot! Holding A♥ 4♥ with a 3 and a 6, I raised in last position, although I normally do not raise at loose Omaha with A 3 holdings. The pot was then duly capped out by "revenge raisers," and we had nine-way action.

The flop came J♥ 3♥ and a 7. With two draws, I went along for the ride, and the betting was capped out after the flop with seven-way action. A bad king turned on fourth street, but I was committed to call the three double bets in five-way action. Note that a high heart would give me the whole pot.

The last card was the 5♥, which gave me nut high and a second-nut low. Four callers called my raise before the showdown. I certainly expected to split the pot with one or more A 2s. But there were mostly highs and one A 4—so I was forced to accept three-quarters of the pot, six huge stacks of chips.

On the thirtieth and sometimes twenty-ninth hand of each tournament, the betting was capped out by the four or five "also rans" remaining, in an effort to pool their non-winning resources into a significant number of chips. Twice I sat out the last-hand festivities with hands that would have lost and was bypassed in the winner's circle by the lucky winner of the last hand.

Given the skill level and the present payoff structure (where the house keeps a greater percentage than in most other forms of gambling) of these games, it was very difficult to be a winner in the long run. So essentially, when you play at a place like this, you are paying for entertainment.

## CAPPELLETTI IN HOLLYWOOD

Hollywood, Florida, that is, and it's about a half-hour north of Miami. It's the home of one of Florida's large Seminole Indian casinos which has, in my opinion, probably the best public poker conditions in Florida. As I noted in the last section, the Tampa Seminole casino has poker tournaments in which it returns only 73% of the buy-in money. At the Hollywood Seminole Casino, believe it or not, they return all of the buy-in money! There is an optional thirty dollar rebuy, which they keep, resulting in roughly a twenty percent drop—however, it seems more psychologically palatable.

I played in three $100 Omaha high-low mini-tournaments, each forty-five hands, and each lasting about an hour-and-a-half. The ten-player prizes were $500-$250-$150-$100 for first through fourth. The nine-player prizes were $450-$225-$125-$100.

Each player starts with $500 in tournament chips. Blinds start at $25 and $10, and they escalate twice at fifteen-hand intervals, so they're $100 and $50 (stakes were $100/$200) for the last fifteen hands. Each player was allowed to make one $30 rebuy (or add-on) of $1,000 in tournament chips! During the three tournaments I played in, only one player declined the bargain rebuy.

During the first tournament, I did not win a pot or a half-pot. But three more-active players exited before me. I came in second in both subsequent tournaments, so I collected $225 and $250, which meant that I showed a slight profit for the session. I believe that a very skillful Omaha high-low player can show a long-run profit of about $20+ per hour playing in this structure—he has to win about 20-30% of the time and finish in the top four most of the time. That probably means that a medium-good Omaha player can go slightly plus—or at least pay very little for his entertainment.

One of the crucial skills necessitated by this format is the ability to judge when to get involved in the last hand shenanigans, after the last hand they count up chips to determine the winner. On the last hand of the third tournament that I played in, with the five players remaining holding approximately $3900, $3500, $3300 (me), $2800 and $1500, I picked up pocket kings suited with a 5 and a deuce. Only the $3500 folded, and the $1500 hand raised, as expected, before the flop to $200.

It was four-way action, and the flop came J 10 4 offsuit. The $1500 blind hand bet the $100, the $2800 (now $2600) hand folded, I called, and the chip leader called, probably a dubious call, since he then couldn't call after fourth street without going below $3500.

The fourth card was the intriguing 3♠, which gave me both a king-high flush draw and a two-way straight wheel draw (2 3 4 5). The $1500 (now $1000) blind bet the $200, I called, and the chip leader (now with $3600) folded. Note that by getting involved at all, the chip leader squandered what could have been a very key $300.

The river card was a very disappointing 5 off-suit. The blind bet $200 at me. The 5, with the 4 and the 3, might have straightened him or given him a low. Could I afford to call this last $200 on my pair of kings?

If I called, I would be down to about $2600 and roughly even with the lowest of the three men sitting out. A key strategy in these mini-tournaments is to finish at least third or fourth to avoid losing $100. If I called and lost, it would be a photo finish as to whether I came in fourth ($100) or fifth (no money).

The blind now had $800 in front of him. If I called and lost, he would win a $1,900 pot, which would give him $2700 and me $2600. But if I folded, I would retain $2800 and he would have only $2500, just short of the money. So I would take third. But if I called and won high, I would have $2600 plus $950 ($3550) and squeeze out the $3500 for second place (losing first by a mere $50!) And if I won the whole pot, I would win first place!

With the 3 4 5 on the board, what are my chances of winning the whole pot?

Suppose I also tell you that my opponent had not looked at his cards yet! He made all his bets blindly because of his pitiful situation. His four cards were still face down in front of him, he was right to force action since he had nothing to lose. What would you do with my pair of kings? Fold and take the sure $150 for third, or go for the berries?

Since precise counting was not allowed at this point, I scanned the stack of the player with approximately $2600 and estimated that I had a couple extra quarter chips, but I was not certain. Since I thought I might win fourth anyway, I called. The other players were understandably tense as he slowly turned over his cards one at a time. He had a low, but my kings beat his 10s for high. Thus I finished second ($250)—just 75 chip dollars out of first and about 50 chip dollars ahead of third, who was understandably annoyed.

Later, on my return flight, I used Caro's Poker Probe on my laptop to determine that my hand with the given board (J 10 5 4 3) rated to win high about 40% of the time against a random hand, but that about half of that time the random hand would get a low split. Thus, roughly, if by calling I would win first about one-fifth of the time, win second, about one-fifth of the time, and win fourth about 60% of the remaining time, then calling was the correct play (roughly $180 to $150). Fascinating stuff!

All in all, although these Omaha high-low mini-tournaments might at first glance appear to be wild and woolly rodeo rides, clearly they also involve substantial amounts of skill and judgment.

# 9 SOME ADDITIONAL THOUGHTS

## GO OMAHA YOUNG MAN

If Horace Greeley were alive today, he might well recommend Omaha high-low as the best opportunity in poker. Why? Because large numbers of Omaha high-low players can actually win at it.

Note that I am referring to the vast majority of Omaha high-low games spread in this country which are of the loose variety, especially those at the lower stakes, $10/$20 and below. I am not referring to the few, usually higher stake, tight Omaha high-low games, at which the play is quite different! My definition of loose ("Cappelletti's Rule") is any table where more than five players are seeing the flop on average. In loose Omaha high-low, there is extra money in most pots, which means that the better hands will show extra profit in the long run.

Is Omaha high-low a very skillful form of poker? Quite the contrary! Most Omaha high-low experts understand that their edge over good-medium level players is rather thin at loose Omaha high-low. But both experts and medium level Omaha high-low players have a considerable edge over the weaker players! That is probably one reason why loose Omaha high-low is becoming so popular with the vast population of medium players. The weaker players love loose Omaha high-low because there is so much action that it is very engrossing and entertaining. For a fuller discussion of these fish-versus-fisherman concepts see the opening perspective of my book *Cappelletti on Omaha*.

The two most significant reasons why medium players do so much better at Omaha high-low than at hold 'em or seven-stud are:

• The basic strategy of Omaha high-low is relatively easy to understand and apply
• The medium players win much more from the weaker players than they surrender to the better players.

The basic strategy or formula for playing Omaha high-low is essentially this: play only good starting hands, continue after the flop only with high-percentage holdings, and don't get caught in big betting on the last two double rounds. Because this basic strategy is straightforward and relatively easy to apply, almost anyone can win at Omaha high-low.

Why do experts have less of an advantage at loose Omaha high-low? In most forms of poker (including high Omaha, hold 'em and seven-card stud), much of the expert's edge results from the expert's ability to make accurate and sophisticated judgments. But in Omaha high-low, because of the bi-directionality, many critical judgments must be based on ambiguous and less accurate information, such as what your various opponents are likely to be holding. Less accurate information yields less accurate judgments and less skill advantage.

Although there often are significant bluff possibilities in straight high pots, there are very few bluffing opportunities in two-way pots, especially when they're well-attended. Also, in well-attended pots in Omaha high-low, it is not always clear whether check, bet, or raise is the most effective action. To put all this another way, Omaha high-low has a lot of randomness—which of course lessens the impact of an expert's skill.

But here is the really good news: those of us who sometimes bother to keep records have noticed that our hourly average win rate playing this Omaha high-low nonsense just happens to be about two to three big bets per hour!! That is roughly double what is widely held to be the average hourly win rate at hold 'em—one to one-and-a-half big bets per hour, although somewhat greater in many low level loose games.

Thus, if a good-medium player does average two big bets per hour at Omaha high-low and only one big bet per hour at hold 'em, then, for any given session, he rates to win as much playing Omaha high-low as he does playing hold 'em at twice the stakes. And because he is playing for lower stakes with less variance, he needs a smaller bankroll since he loses less often and his occasional big loss is less than half as much.

Notwithstanding all of this good news, there is also some bad news! Is Omaha so frustrating at times that you might even lose your sense of humor? Yes! But is Omaha fun to play? Again yes! Why is that bad? Warning: Omaha is dangerously addictive! You too may become an Omaholic!

## OMAHA VERSUS HOLD 'EM

For many years I have been listening to Omaholics complain about bad beats, last cards, etc. But somehow the game has at least tripled in popularity, and those who complain the loudest are still found at the Omaha tables. Why?

I believe that it is easier to win at Omaha high or even Omaha high-low than at hold 'em—mainly because very few players can play Omaha correctly. Even most "medium-to-good" Omaha players cost themselves money by playing incorrectly both before and after the flop. Add that better-player money to what the several weak players in the game contribute and there is ample money to be won. Note that even the weak players win more often, and hence they are more likely to keep coming back.

In many hold 'em games, especially at higher stakes, many of the medium and better players play reasonably well. Even if these reasonable players deviate somewhat from what you consider to be the optimum hold 'em strategy, sometimes their variations or instinctive plays are based on table situations, of which you may be unaware, and hence these plays may actually be equal or superior to what you believe is the correct play. There is always the possibility that your perception of reality is slightly off.

When too many of your opponents are playing a reasonable hold 'em formula, it has a noticeable negative impact on your results. If about half or more of the players play well enough to win a little or break even, your hourly rate of winning, minus the time dollars or rake, probably drops to less than what you rate to win in a lower-stake, more favorable game. To put this another way, if too many of your opponents are generally playing the same tight-aggressive textbook hold 'em formula, even if you think they play somewhat inferior to you, they may well be taking money out of the game rather than putting money in. Even if there are several weak players feeding the game, most of your equity is from weak-player confrontations and there is less overall money in that game. The more winning players who rate to take money out of a game, the less you win.

How does skill fit into this picture? I have often been asked whether hold 'em or Omaha is the more skillful game. Are apples or oranges more colorful? The two games entail different types of skill. Poker skill is a combination of intelligence and sensitivity. It takes intelligence to recognize and evaluate objective card situations, such as possible holdings and percentages of winning. It takes sensitivity to judge opponents.

Hold 'em hands have only two cards. Most hold 'em hands completely miss the flop about two-thirds of the time. If your opponents have missed the flop, the pot is up for grabs—and it might as well be you who grabs it's long as you do not try to grab too often. Often someone else also tries grabbing, and a lot of fancy maneuvering occurs. Hold 'em is the more skillful game from the standpoint of sensitivity, reading your opponents, judging their likely holdings, and playing your position, which position is more significant in hold 'em.

Each four-card Omaha hand has six two-card combinations. At Omaha, someone holds the nuts about ten times more frequently than at hold 'em and more players stay in to see the flop! There are many variations, themes and delicate situations at Omaha. To truly optimize your play, considerable skill is required to evaluate the various potentials of a given hand both objectively, estimating your odds, and subjectively, relative to your opponents and momentum of the game. Complicated evaluations favor those with greater intelligence and better mental processing faculties. Note that many Omaha players do not realize that there are complicated evaluations involved.

If you could judge your opponent's probable holdings at Omaha as well as you can at hold 'em, then Omaha would probably entail more overall skill. But you can't! At Omaha, your opponent not only has the two-card holding that he is playing, but he also might have several other prospects with his two additional cards. At Omaha high-low, there is even more uncertainty. Thus, a good player at hold 'em has a much better read on his opponents than a good player at Omaha has. There is much skill involved in reading your opponents and using that information, especially when you have a positional advantage.

In ascertaining the overall skill content of hold 'em and Omaha, the mathematical niceties at Omaha (for example, making a 55% play instead of a 45% play) are probably not as significant as stealing default pots at hold 'em. There is probably more poker skill involved at hold 'em than at Omaha. However, which game inherently has more skill is not as consequential, in limit poker, as upon which game does your skill have the greatest impact!

Having a slightly greater skill advantage in a hold 'em game where many players are folding bad hands will probably not gain you as many dollars as you gain in an Omaha game where seven players are seeing the flop! Horace Greeley advised, "Go west young man," for many of the same reasons as I advise you to play Omaha.

It is not unusual to find an Omaha game where more than half the players are seeing every flop. It is not unusual to find an Omaha game where three or more callers, often the same ones from hand to hand, call after the flop. In such games, you are usually well paid off when you win. It is certainly preferable to play in a game in which more players are contributing, rather than to struggle in a game in which a lot of players are doing the same thing.

## LOVED OR FEARED?

The Machiavellian question, "whether it is better to be loved or feared," bears profoundly on your image at the poker table. Being "feared" alludes to a generally tight player who usually has sound values for his bets and raises; hence, when he bets, other players tend to fold. Being "loved" alludes to a generally loose aggressive player who often bets on very little; hence, other players strain to call his bets. It is my considered opinion that one of the key strategic differences between hold 'em and Omaha is that, normally, in hold 'em it is better to be feared, whereas in Omaha it is better to be loved.

In an average hold 'em game, a tightish (feared) but aggressive expert tends to win on average about one-and-a-half big bets per hour, for example, about $30 per hour at $10/$20. Unless there are abnormalities at the table, no loose player (loved) can win more than that on average. In a very loose hold 'em game, certain aggressive strategies geared to certain bad players might average about twice that rate—but extremely favorable conditions would be required.

It is difficult to find a "not loose or tight" high Omaha game. When you do find one, however, you'll see that a tightish expert tends to win less than the one-and-a-half big bets per hour as there are fewer default pot opportunities in Omaha. The average Omaha game tends to be generally loose, because most players call too frequently before and after the flop. Optimal expert play in most high Omaha games should yield more than two big bets per hour.

What constitutes optimal expert play in loose high Omaha games? Is it analogous to hold 'em—in which the tightish expert usually plays only great hands in early seats and occasionally fools around in late seats? Although the positional advantage for default pots in Omaha is clearly less than in hold 'em, position in Omaha is very crucial to building big pots, both before and after the flop. That fact affects your competitive focus. For example, you see the flop with lesser hands in late position because you have better prospects of raising after a good flop.

In Omaha the dominant factor is the big payoff potential! Whereas skillfully fighting in the trenches for smaller pots is a significant part of your overall win, these smaller pots are not a result of your engineering; you deal with them routinely as they come along. Your main strategy and objective in high Omaha is to promote occasional big pots, by raising before the flop, in which you have better chances of winning the last card roulette than the other players.

If you tend to get many callers when you have these good hands, you collect a big payoff when you do win. If you can win one or two big pots per session, and several lesser pots, and generally keep your losses down, you will certainly be in the plus column. And, if you happen to win one or more additional big pots during any given session, your hourly rate will increase tremendously.

To put this discussion another way, the dollars won in big pots is usually the dominant portion of a winner's net at high Omaha. If that big pot contribution is enhanced because more players love to call your bets and raises, then your bread is buttered even better.

## POSITIONAL RAISE IN OMAHA HIGH-LOW

Although position in Omaha high-low may not be as important as it is in hold 'em, mainly because there are fewer default pots in Omaha, position is generally more important in Omaha high-low than it is in straight high Omaha, especially when delicate involvement decisions have to be made after the flop. Acting last with good holdings after the flop makes more money in both games. But acting last with medium to marginal holdings in high-low both saves more money than in straight high Omaha, and also allows for occasional opportunistic involvements, that would be anti-percentage in an early seat. Note that whenever you are sitting in last seat in any flop game after the flop, each time you hear an earlier player check, your equity in the pot increases.

# SOME ADDITIONAL THOUGHTS

I was playing at $5/$10 Omaha high-low at the Taj Mahal in Atlantic City. In last position, I called a raise before the flop made by the player directly in front of me. I held A♠ 8♥ 7♠ 2♥. One blind folded, and the three other players called. The pot held $55. The flop came K♥ J♥ 7♣. The first three players checked to the before-the-flop raiser on my right, who bet.

I was not quite good enough to call, but, because of the first three checks and my last position, I raised! I have always called this tactic a "positional raise"—you are raising more on position than on cards.

The other three players folded, and the bettor called. The fourth card was the 5♠, which gave me a draw at lock low. My low draws were probably lessened because of probable low cards in the three hands that saw the flop and folded. My opponent checked to me, so I made the obligatory bet, just in case he also had nothing and felt like folding. He called.

The last card was the 5♥, pairing the board and giving me a low flush. He checked to me again and I made a friendly check, since this type of thin bet rates to lose more than it gains. He had raised on four big cards and merely had top two, so my junk flush scooped the pot.

Some of the other players laughed at my raise when they saw my hand. But my raise, many times better than a call, had a lot going for it. Because of my position, I had seen the other three players check! Unless someone was trapping with trips or had a great draw, their folding was likely. Most Omaha high-low players are programmed to avoid getting involved in potentially big betting with medium cards.

Clearly my raise got rid of speculative holdings like jack and another heart. Admittedly, even one additional caller would seriously reduce the value of my junk flush draw, which unfortunately was my major asset.

But I did have some other minor prospects. I make a low about one-tenth of the time, and, who knows, trip 7s or aces-over might even win. Do not undervalue the often sizable chances, sometimes as high as 50%, that the bettor will fold now or after fourth or fifth street. Bet if you feel that he needed a good last card.

In this situation, my raise also served as an inhibitory raise, and it would be quite likely that the fourth card betting would get checked around to me, even if one of the callers had something, which would thus give me the option of getting a free fifth card. But, if there was even one other caller, it would probably be anti-percentage to make the usual fourth round follow through bet, which is generally made because speculators tend to fold the fourth round double-sized bet, since anyone calling the raise cold is probably not speculating.

The overall bottom line was that I invested $10, and later $10 more, and ended up making $75. If all likely possibilities were listed and evaluated, I believe that my raise was probably operating well within the odds. Note how often it is correct to raise an after-the-flop bettor on your right in Omaha, especially when you are in last position.

## BIG MOVES AT HIGH-LOW

Omaha high-low appears to be growing in popularity faster than any other poker game. Many of us badmouth the game and think it is one of the least skillful poker games primarily because our judgment of opponent's holdings is much less accurate and because of the bi-directionality. However, there are certainly some skillful general strategies involved in Omaha high-low, not the least of which is finding a table where one or more players are essentially giving away money. If all players at the table are playing reasonably sound, an expert has only a small edge.

Optimum strategy for Omaha high-low depends on whether a given table is mostly a fish game or a quality game. If a game has too much quality, you should not be playing in it—unless your objective is entertainment. A good game is not a good game.

If you are fortunate enough to be playing in a fishy game in which many players get involved in most of the hands, your primary strategy is to play good cards and bet as much as you can on good flops. Whenever you have a winning hand, you get more of the loose extra money. Skillful subtleties, bluffing, and intimidation are mostly for flare, image, and to "keep 'em coming."

Anyone can win with a big hand. It takes macho skill, experience, and luck to win with lesser hands. But it takes even more skill to know when not to lose extra money by being over-active! In a tightish, conservative quality game environment, you should make big moves more frequently, especially early in the session, than you should in loose games, not only to win the current pot, but also to enhance your image as a tough speculator.

What are big moves? Good players are conservative about calling after the flop, and ultra-conservative about calling a raise on the turn, where the limit doubles. You can exploit those sound tendencies by making well-timed bets or raises, which often cause sound players to fold marginal holdings that would beat your marginal holdings. Many of these big moves are surprisingly more profitable in a tight game than in a looser game, where they get called more often. And, as in loose games, big moves in tight games help perpetuate an illusion of wild, speculative play. It helps to recognize certain opportunistic situations where percentages favor the big mover, for example:

• **The Positional Raise**. You have medium two-way prospects, and a loose bettor leads on your right. A raise might drop most or all of the remaining players and give you good odds of getting half of the pot—and a check to you on fourth street. For a further discussion of this see the previous section.

• **The Promo Raise.** You have a third-rate high or low holding that might win if a second-rate holding folds because of the heat. These raises are actually sound, rather than speculative, if you have good prospects—draws or possible winners in the other direction (see Chapter 4).

• **The Amplified Bet.** You check in first seat, and the player on your left bets the flop. Several players, including you, limp in. The fourth card gives you dubious chances of winning both high and low. If you bet, the player on your left is often anxious to raise and might well pressure everybody else out. The pot is big enough to risk calling one-on-one.

• **Flop Bluffing.** Basic principles tell us that if a bet of one unit will win an N unit pot one out of N times, the bet is sound regardless of holdings. If you have some chance of winning the pot by betting after the flop and some chance of actually drawing a winning hand, the combination of those two possibilities often makes betting a sound investment. Note that calling does not gain the initiative or the folding factor advantages. Some specific examples:

**1. The high bluff**—In most games, there are more low hands seeing the flop than high hands. When the flop has two high cards, you should occasionally bet it with a less-than-adequate high, especially if you have a tight image, and preferably when you also have some secondary draws. You often get just one caller. If the fourth card is helpful or strong that is, gives board pair, flush or straight, you might try betting one more time.

**2. Acey-deucy ("cretin's delight")**—The flop contains an ace and a deuce. You happen to have any two other low cards. Most 3 4 holdings without an ace or deuce should not have seen the flop. Bet the flop proudly, as if you have 3 4, and watch most of the other low hands fold. The most likely caller is a high contender, beware—he might also have a better low. It helps to get a good turn card! This is usually a good time to solicit a friendly check out.

**3. Ugly straight flop**—The flop contains a medium high straight like J 10 7 or Q 10 8. Nobody plays a 9 8 or J 9? Bet the flop with any pair and two-card low draw. The most likely non-fish caller might have trips or flush draw and will probably fold if the board doesn't pair or flush.

Over the years, I've mentioned many big moves at high-low. I have received considerable correspondence either exalting them or complaining about how some of these big moves worked or didn't work. There are no guarantees in Omaha high-low! Remember, much of the value in making these big moves is that you get more action when you really have the goods.

## HOW GOOD IS ABC AT POT LIMIT?

Hands containing an A 2 3 (ABC hands) are among the best hands in loose limit Omaha high-low. But how good are ABCs at tight pot limit? Let's look at an example situation.

Early in a pot-limit Omaha high-low tournament, you pick up an A 2 3 J with the jack and deuce, both diamonds. The blinds are $10 and $15. You're in first seat, and you smooth-call the $15 because low hands pay off better with lots of company.

There is one other $15 crawler in back of you, and then the button raises $35, making it fifty to go. The small blind folds, and the big blind calls. What do you do?

Unless you are a fan of domination mind games, you should just call. You are content with the raise, and you do not want anyone else to fold. If one of the other three players has an A 2 or an A 3, you are barely ahead of the percentages. If you run a simulation with your hand versus a hand containing an A 2 and two random hands, your hand wins merely about 29% of the time (25% is average, see Omaha Average Explanation Chart). And if either of the two random hands happens to contain an A 3 or 2 3, your expectations are about average.

It's now four-way action (with $210 in pot), and the flop comes a 5 7 10 rainbow. The big-blind leads with $100. What should you do?

Do not make the mistake of thinking that two low cards on the flop make you a favorite to win money. Although this ABC hand will now make a nut low about 72% of the time, some of your lows will be tied and you will receive only a quarter or a sixth of the pot. And since you have very little chance of winning high, you are actually a slight percentage underdog in this hand! That means that you are calling because you will lose less in the long run by calling than by folding. Thus, you do not want to increase your investment.

So you call, the crawler in back of you folds, and the button, who raised before the flop, calls. It is interesting to stop here and note what would happen if you ran a simulation with this flop and three hands: your hand, a second hand with an A 2 and two other random cards, and a third hand with all four random cards. The random hand would win the most—about 37% of the time! The A 2 hand would win about 33% of the time (average), and your hand would win about 30% of the time.

The turn card is the offsuit queen (four suits on board—no flushes this hand). A bit of good news is that you now have a nut gut straight draw. But the bad news is that you have not made your low yet, which is now about 48% to make as there are 21 out of 44 cards remaining.

The player in first seat bets $200! Since your low expectation is about one-fourth of the pot (win half about one-half of the time), you call. And a king would probably scoop the whole pot.

The last card is an 8. At least you made a nut low and will get some money back. The first player goes all-in with his remaining 400+ chips. You must call, as does the before-the-flop raiser—who also has an A 2. The first player proudly tables his J 10 9 8 for half the pot. You get back about $580 of the $760 you put in. Unlucky.

When you have an ABC hand, most fourth cards will make a hand without strong high potential. Since most pot-limit pots involve only a few players, a lack of high potential seriously reduces the effectiveness of going low. Note that a pot-sized bet on the turn often makes even the best low draws unprofitable. That usually suggests a strategy of not raising early and keeping the pot size smaller, until you actually make your nut low.

But if you do make a nut low early—on the turn or the flop—especially when you also have the extension card, the 3 in the above hand allows you to keep the nut low even if an ace or deuce appears on the last card, i.e. it's uncounterfeitable, then it is often right to pressure the non-nut high players. If you have some high potential, such as a high pair, then you might make pot-sized bets or raises, and risk getting quartered, to muscle out the non-nut highs. It is not unusual for one of the two nut lows to win high with a small pair.

All in all, although an ABC hand is obviously a good starting hand in any kind of Omaha high-low game, you must understand that the potential value of low is proportional to the number of players in the pot.

## THE "DOOMSDAY BET"

While playing in the middle stages of a pot-limit Omaha high-low tournament, in small blind I picked up a 2♣ 4♣ 6♥ 8♥. With six players calling the pot, it was clear to call the extra $25. Note that in "Blind Fishing" (see Chapter 3), I stated that calling a half-bet blind in a well attended pot was quite clear with a 2 and a 4 and that having a 6 also made it even better.

The flop came an unimpressive J 7 3 rainbow. I certainly would fold any sizable bet. Roughly 45% of the time there would be an A 2 lurking; about 70% of the time there would be either an A 2 or an A 4. I checked, the player on my left bet $75, and three other players called around to me. Since there was a fair amount of money already in the pot, I called and hoped for an ace, which would give me a nut low, or the gut 5.

The turn card was the very impressive 5♥ which gave me the current nut high. It also happened to give me a two-way straight flush draw as the 7 in the flop was a heart. And the 5 also gave me a third-nut low, behind A 2 and A 4, which might be very significant if no A 2s were present.

# SOME ADDITIONAL THOUGHTS

Although a low straight is very fragile and it can easily lose on a last card which pairs the board or makes a flush or higher straight, nevertheless, at pot limit, it is often right to go for it and bet the pot with the nut high straight. It is clearly correct to bet the pot if that takes most of your chips, since you do not have to fear a big bet if a scary card appears on the river. And, finally, in this particular situation, it was certainly right to move, since my bet might pressure out an A 4 or another 2 4, which would give me low if there were no A 2s.

So I bet the $700+ pot, which took slightly more than half of my remaining chips. If no one had an A 2, I might even win the whole pot right now.

But I got not one, but two callers. Probably one or both of them had an A 2—or perhaps there was another 4 6, and I would get quartered. The second caller thought a bit, as if he were perhaps considering a raise.

The river card was the 10♠. If someone held a 9 8, that would make a jack-high straight, which would beat my 7-high straight. So there I was in first position with second-best high and third-best low.

What would you do if you were there in my seat with about $600 in chips in front of you, looking at a $2,900 pot? Note that betting your $600 would probably not make an A 4 or 2 4 player fold (he'd just called your $700+ bet).

Nevertheless, this is actually a very clear bet-it-all "Doomsday Bet" situation. At pot-limit high-low, it was correct to bet my remaining $600. If I checked and someone else bet, I would certainly have to call on pot value, since it was not that likely that a 9 8 was out, and the other bettor might well be pushing a nut low (and marginal high).

Certainly, if someone did hold a 9 8, he would make a big bet (more than my remaining chips). Thus, if someone had the 9 8, I was doomed anyway, so I might as well bet just in case I still had a winner.

Yup. They both had to call with their A 2s, so I won half of the big pot and nearly doubled my chip holdings.

There is often a considerable amount of skill in judging when you are likely to be on the right side of things and then play to optimize your winnings. All too frequently at Omaha high-low, we find ourselves on the wrong side—helplessly getting quartered with our A 2s.

## NO-LIMIT OMAHA HIGH-LOW

Several years ago, in the final stages of an Omaha high-low tournament aboard a cruise ship, I played no-limit Omaha high-low for the first time. Furthermore, I actually liked it!

Although I have played a lot of pot-limit high Omaha, I have always felt that pot-limit or no-limit Omaha high-low must be a crap shoot. Quite the contrary. No-limit Omaha high-low is not much worse than no-limit hold 'em when it comes down to crap shooting.

The following hand taught me an interesting principle that applies when winning three-quarters of the pot is reasonably likely. In big blind ($200) I picked up A♦ 4♦, an 8, and a *jack*. At that point, I was the chip leader at my table—I had about $10,000 in chips. The next highest player, with about $9,000 in chips, who frequently had been raising before the flop, made it $400 to go. I was the only caller, defending my blind.

The flop came 3 6 7 off-suit with one diamond. My opponent, who had a tendency to make small bets, bet $400. I called with my second-nut low.

The fourth card was the 10♥, and he bet another $400. I called.

The last card was the 9♥, which gave me a nut high! He bet $500. At that point, he had about $7,000 left. How much should I have raised?

With this particular opponent, it was difficult to judge whether he was betting slow out of habit or baiting me with a great hand. But since I rated to get at least half the pot, at worst I would have been quartered if he held exactly A 2 8 J. This now became a problem of extraction—how much to raise—given that I wanted to get called!

Since he had committed only $1,700 to the pot at that point, he might well have folded if I had pushed my stack. But I did not want to bait him with a small raise, since I probably would not get reraised—unless he had half the pot locked with an A 2. So the question was: what was he most likely to have, and how much would he be willing to call?

Since he had raised before the flop into traffic, he probably had an ace because almost all Omaha high-low raising hands have an ace. If he also had a deuce, nothing mattered, since we would split. But if he had an 8-other (making lower straights) or a 5 4 without an ace, he might call anything.

I finally chose to raise him a tempting $2,000, which is about what I might raise if I were bluffing and enough to fold a medium-to-bad hand but not a disaster if I ran into a lock. He thought about it for a while, and then he called with his A 3 3 4, trips and an A 4 low. So I ended up winning three-quarters of the pot—a net win of about $2,000.

It was then that I noted in retrospect that if I had foreseen the possibility of winning three-quarters of the pot, I had not bet enough! If I had bet more, $3,000, for example, I would have netted more if he had called, but if he had folded, I would have won about the same $2,000 which was the whole pot—the $1,700 he would have folded and the blinds. To put this another way, his calling my $2,000 bet cost him very little.

Thus, in no-limit Omaha high-low, when both your high and low holdings can be tied, winning three-quarters of the pot is a foreseeable likely result. In such a situation, you should raise an adequate amount such that three-quarters of the pot if called would net you considerably more than the whole pot if folded.

## BACKSTAGE

I was sitting beside one of my advanced poker students at a $10/$20 Omaha high-low table at the Taj in Atlantic City. She was watching me try to pump as many chips as possible into a pot in which I held an A 2 6 9, and the flop, an 8 7 5, had given me the nut straight and the nut low draw.

I continued firing into five-way action after a 3 hit the turn, as I now had both the nut high and the nut low. There were three callers, and the other A 2 raised. I reraised. The pot was huge.

There were two clubs on the board. The river card was the deuce of clubs, the "deuce of death"—the only card which shipped both of my locks down the drain.

As we watched the two huge half pots being pushed towards the club-flush and the A 4, I methodically said my usual, "Nice hand" to the winners. My student whispered to me, "How can you stand it?!"

So I told her that there is not only a correct way to play every hand, but also a correct way to act and react after the hand is over. And that option one, as always, was simply to congratulate the winners and just go on to the next hand. That's what I usually do. But there are other options.

"Like what?" she asked.

"Well, not all good players take the, let's call it the 'stoical' approach. There are some good players who prefer to play various psychological games. For example, there are those who act like they're going on tilt."

"Try to picture this. Suppose I was one of those emotive players who are inclined to put on a show (some seem to be trying for an Academy Award). First, as soon as the winning hands were seen, I might throw my hand face-up on the table so that everyone could see the two former locka-locka cards. Then I would say something either nasty or sarcastic to the winners. Then I might signal for the cocktail waitress that I need another drink. Note that I might not really be drinking. I might be ordering Bloody Mary mix without vodka, or tonic without gin, etc. Then, I might play one of the first marginal hands that came along, and then show it with great pride. I might even stick in an extra aggressive raise before or just after the flop.

She interrupted, "But what does all this accomplish?"

I said, "Well, disguising your play is even more fruitful at Omaha than at hold 'em. I reminded her of the basic principle that in loose Omaha it is better to be loved than feared. That is, you make more money by getting extra callers than you do by stealing default pots." Note that this does not apply to hold 'em—in that game it is usually better to be feared than loved.

"So," I told her, "Since one likes to get more callers in Omaha, it is actually profitable to adopt various deceptive strategies, the overall purpose of which is to get more players into your pots."

She perceptively asked, "So is all this considered ethical?"

"Of course," I responded, "In poker, deception is considered part of the game. You might think of this as simply a variation of the grand old poker strategem of luring in players who think they are playing against weak opponents. Back in the old days of Mississippi riverboats, it was not uncommon for certain professional gamblers to act drunk so that tourists would think they were easy marks."

"Well, then, if this is ethical and also advantageous, then why don't you do it?"

"Just call it personal preference," I answered. My feelings on this subject are probably affected by years of playing tournament bridge, in which "coffee housing" is considered unethical. Then I conceded, "I've tried it a few times—it seems to work. But what about you? Are you interested in the performing arts?"

She smiled sweetly, "Why do you think I always have a lot of chips in front of me?"

# 10 POOR CAPPELLETTI'S ALMANAC

Many of the bridge and poker articles I have written over the years have contained "words of wisdom" that sound like old sayings—except that I might have been the first person to say them. It is never clear who first says anything, though. For example, my first useful rule, written in a high school essay about misplacing things, was "If you can't find something, look under something." It must have been said before by somebody.

As a closing to this book, for your consideration and review, some of my poker words to live by are featured on the following page:

# POOR CAPPELLETTI'S ALMANAC

**1.** Aggressiveness pays in most games, including love, war, and poker.

**2.** When you are playing good poker, you are folding a lot.

**3.** If you want to win a lot at Omaha, you have to bet a lot.

**4.** Whereas it might be better to be "feared" at hold 'em, it is clearly better to be "loved" at Omaha. (Note this one!)

**5.** You learn a lot more from losing than from winning.

**6.** When losing, change tables.

**7.** Thou shalt not thin-bet the last card unless it is a brick.

**8.** In poker tournaments, most of the time do only what the cards and chips tell you to do; don't do what you don't have to do.

*When you leave the poker table, you might try these also:*

**9.** Don't change good plans without good reasons.

**10.** If you want to be successful at political endeavors, people have to think, at worst, that you are a good guy.

**11.** Reformed crooks are sometimes the most honest people.

**12.** You have truly made it, if you have enjoyed making it.

**13.** Those who ask "why" have been superceded by those who ask "why not."

*And finally, a controversial mathematical theorem:*

**14.** If a person is N minutes late, she is even-money to be twice N minutes late.

# 11 GLOSSARY

**ABC:** A four-card Omaha hand that contains an ace, deuce and three and any other card.

**ABCD:** a four-card Omaha hand consisting of an ace, deuce, three and four.

**Ante:** in many poker games (not Omaha), players each pay a small amount to start a pot.

**Backdoor flush:** three cards of same suit needing two cards of that suit to make flush.

**Backdoor straight:** three cards needing two appropriate cards to make straight (ex. 5 6 8 needs 4 7 or 7 9).

**Before the flop:** the initial round of betting which occurs before the flop

**Before the flop raiser:** a raiser of the first round of betting

**Bicycle:** An ace through five straight; the best low hand at Omaha high-low, with high scooping possibilities as well.

**Blind:** a forced initial wager in the first round of betting, most often one small and then one large bet by the first two players to act.

**Blind bet:** A bet made by a player who hasn't looked at his cards

**Board, board cards:** In hold 'em or Omaha, the five exposed communal cards

**Bricked:** Same as counterfeited

**Button:** A button-size plastic marker which indicates the dealers position.

**Call:** When one player makes a bet, another player *calls* by putting in an equal amount.

**Caller:** A player who calls the current bet.

**Calling cold:** A hand that enters the pot by calling a bet *and* a raise

**Calling station:** A weak player who calls too many bets.

**Cap:** A round of betting where no more raises are allowed because the maximum number of raises has been reached. (Most house rules allow three raises.)

**Check:** With no bet due, a player chooses to bet nothing.

**Check and raise:** A trapping ploy; instead of betting, a player checks and then raises if someone else bets, thereby getting two bets per player into the pot instead of one

**Counterfeited:** When one of a players two low hand cards, appears on board.

**Couple:** Any two cards in a four-card Omaha hand.

**Dead cards:** In seven card stud, previously seen cards that are known not to be in the deck

**Drive:** To make the lead (first) bet on several consecutive rounds of betting

**Eleven-handed:** Eleven players in a pot or game

**Fish:** A sucker, a weak player who usually loses

**Fishing:** Taking an action which tends to attract a weaker player into the pot

**Fishing in:** Investing money in a pot with a dubious return.

**Fourth, Fifth Street:** The 4$^{th}$ and 5$^{th}$ (last) board cards in Omaha are called 4$^{th}$ street and 5$^{th}$ street.

**Flop:** In hold 'em or Omaha, the first three board cards exposed simultaneously.

**Flush draw:** Four cards of the same suit needing a fifth

card of that suit to make a flush.

**Free card:** When betting is checked around, all players get a "free" card

**Full table:** A poker table with players in all seats (usually 8-11 players).

**Give a free card:** Generally considered a mistake; by failing to bet, a hand that would have folded against a bet, stays in and might improve and become the winner.

**Gutshot:** An inside straight draw.

**Halved:** When two players tie for the pot and each gets one half.

**Heavenly game:** A game with many loose players

**High flop:** In Omaha high low, 2 or 3 high cards (9 or higher) in a three-card flop

**Inside straight draw:** Four cards, needing one inside card (ex. 5 6 7 9 needs 8) to make a straight. Also called a gutshot.

**Killer Games:** A rather complicated action device, most often found at Omaha high low, where stakes are increased for one pot following the scoop of a big pot. An Omaha high/low game with a kill means that whenever someone scoops a big pot, greater than a predesignated size, the stakes either double (called a **full kill**) or in some casinos, increase by 50% (**half kill**) for the next hand only. The scooper is required to ante to increase the starting size of that one kill pot.

Note that when an Omaha game is billed as $10/$20 with a kill that could mean either a full kill or a half kill.

For example, if a player scoops a pot greater than $100 (or in some places less), he must put $10 into the next pot in addition to the regular blinds, which is played at $20/40 limit. If it were a half kill, the next pot would be played at $15/30 limit.

**Live cards:** In Omaha, usually referring to the number of hit cards remaining in the deck

**Lock:** The best hand that can be made from the given board cards.

**Low flop:** In Omaha high low, 2 or 3 low cards (8 or lower) in 3-card flop.

**Nut flush:** The highest flush possible with the given board cards.

**Nut low:** The lowest hand possible with the given board cards. (For example, if the board had 2-4-6-8-J, then an A-3 in the hand would make the nut low, A-2-3-4-6).

**Nut straight:** The highest straight possible with the given board cards

**Nuts, the nuts:** The lock hand..

**Outside straight draw:** Four cards needing either outside card (ex. 5 6 7 8 needs 4 or 9).

**Position:** The order in which players act (fold, call, check or raise), as specified by the dealer button.

**Pull:** A strategy of not betting or betting lesser amounts to keep other players in the pot.

**Push:** A strategy of betting or raising aggressively to pressure other players into folding.

**Quartered:** When two players tie for half the pot and each gets one half or the half, that is, one quarter of the total.

**Rainbow:** Cards all of different suits, usually referring to the three-card flop.

**Raiser:** A player who raises a bet.

**River:** The fifth and last board card; the name of the round.

**Rule game:** An Omaha high low table where an average of five or more players are see the flop—Cappelletti's Rule.

**Scooping:** Winning both the high and the low end of the pot.

**Second best:** A player who loses with second best poker hand.

**Short handed:** A poker table with five or fewer players.

**Showdown:** The exposing of hands after the final bet to determine the winner.

**Split pot:** To divide the pot because of a tie or when playing high low split, where the high and low ends of the pot are split.

**Suited:** Two or more cards of the same suit.

**Ten-handed:** Ten players in a pot or game.

**Trap, trapping:** Checking a good hand to lure other players into betting.

**Trapped:** Having called and lost with a hand that appeared too good to fold.

**Turn:** The fourth board card; the name of the round.

**Two-way straight draw:** An outside straight draw.

**Wheel:** A hand that goes both ways at high low. See bicycle.

# POWERFUL POKER SIMULATIONS
## A MUST FOR SERIOUS PLAYERS WITH A COMPUTER!
IBM compatibles CD ROM Windows 3.1, 95, and 98, ME & XP - Full Color Graphics

**Play interactive poker** against these **incredible** full color poker simulation programs - they're the absolute **best** method to improve game. Computer players act like real players. All games let you set the limits and rake, have fully programmable players, adjustable lineup, stat tracking, and Hand Analyzer for starting hands. MIke Caro, the world's foremost poker theoretician says, "Amazing...A steal for under $500." Includes free telephone support. **New Feature!** - "Smart advisor" gives expert advice for every play in every game!

**1. TURBO TEXAS HOLD'EM FOR WINDOWS - $89.95** - Choose which players, how many, 2-10, you want to play, create loose/tight game, control check-raising, bluffing, position, sensitivity to pot odds, more! Also, instant replay, pop-up odds, Professional Advisor, keeps track of play statistics. Free bonus: Hold'em Hand Analyzer analyzes all 169 pocket hands in detail, their win rates under any conditions you set. Caro says this "hold'em software is the most powerful ever created." Great product!

**2. TURBO SEVEN-CARD STUD FOR WINDOWS - $89.95** - Create any conditions of play; choose number of players (2-8), bet amounts, fixed or spread limit, bring-in method, tight/loose conditions, position, reaction to board, number of dead cards, stack deck to create special conditions, instant replay. Terrific stat reporting includes analysis of starting cards, 3-D bar charts, graphs. Play interactively, run high speed simulation to test strategies. Hand Analyzer analyzes starting hands in detail. Wow!

**3. TURBO OMAHA HIGH-LOW SPLIT FOR WINDOWS - $89.95** -Specify any playing conditions; betting limits, number of raises, blind structures, button position, aggressiveness/passiveness of opponents, number of players (2-10), types of hands dealt, blinds, position, board reaction, specify flop, turn, river cards! Choose opponents, use provided point count or create your own. Statistical reporting, instant replay, pop-up odds, high speed simulation to test strategies, amazing Hand Analyzer, much more!

**4. TURBO OMAHA HIGH FOR WINDOWS - $89.95** - Same features as above, but tailored for the Omaha High-only game. Caro says program is "an electrifying research tool...it can clearly be worth thousands of dollars to any serious player. A must for Omaha High players.

**5. TURBO 7 STUD 8 OR BETTER - $89.95** - Brand new with all the features you expect from the Wilson Turbo products: the latest artificial intelligence, instant advice and exact odds, play versus 2-7 opponents, enhanced data charts that can be exported or printed, the ability to fold out of turn and immediately go to the next hand, ability to peek at opponents hand, optional warning mode that warns you if a play disagrees with the advisor, and automatic testing mode that can run up to 50 tests unattended. Challenge tough computer players who vary their styles for a truly great poker game.

---

## 6. TOURNAMENT TEXAS HOLD'EM - $59.95
Set-up for tournament practice and play, this realistic simulation pits you against celebrity look-alikes. Tons of options let you control tournament size with 10 to 300 entrants, select limits, ante, rake, blind structures, freezeouts, number of rebuys and competition level of opponents - average, tough, or toughest. Pop-up status report shows how you're doing vs. the competition. Save tournaments in progress to play again later. Additional feature allows you to quickly finish a folded hand and go on to the next.

# GREAT POKER BOOKS
## ADD THESE TO YOUR LIBRARY - ORDER NOW!

**TOURNAMENT POKER** by Tom McEvoy - Rated by pros as best book on tournaments ever written, and enthusiastically endorsed by more than 5 world champions, this is a must for every player's library. Packed solid with winning strategies for all 11 games in the World Series of Poker, with extensive discussions of 7-card stud, limit hold'em, pot and no-limit hold'em, Omaha high-low, re-buy, half-half tournaments, satellites, strategies for each stage of tournaments. Big player profiles. 344 pages, paperback, $39.95.

**OMAHA HI-LO POKER** by Shane Smith - Learn essential winning strategies for beating Omaha high-low; the best starting hands, how to play the flop, turn, and river, how to read the board for both high and low, dangerous draws, and how to win low-limit tournaments. Smith shows the differences between Omaha high-low and hold'em strategies. Includes odds charts, glossary, low-limit tips, strategic ideas. 84 pages, 8 x 11, spiral bound, $17.95.

**7-CARD STUD (THE COMPLETE COURSE IN WINNING AT MEDIUM & LOWER LIMITS)** by Roy West - Learn the latest strategies for winning at $1-$4 spread-limit up to $10-$20 fixed-limit games. Covers starting hands, 3rd-7th street strategy for playing most hands, overcards, selective aggressiveness, reading hands, secrets of the pros, psychology, more - in a 42 "lesson" informal format. Includes bonus chapter on 7-stud tournament strategy by World Champion Tom McEvoy. 160 pages, paperback, $24.95.

**POKER TOURNAMENT TIPS FROM THE PROS** by Shane Smith - Essential advice from poker theorists, authors, and tournament winners on the best strategies for winning the big prizes at low-limit re-buy tournaments. Learn the best strategies for each of the four stages of play—opening, middle, late and final—how to avoid 26 potential traps, advice on re-buys, aggressive play, clock-watching, inside moves, top 20 tips for winning tournaments, more. Advice from McEvoy, Caro, Malmuth, Ciaffone, others. 160 pages, $19.95.

**WINNING LOW LIMIT HOLD'EM** by Lee Jones - This essential book on playing 1-4, 3-6, and 1-4-8-8 low limit hold'em is packed with insights on winning: pre-flop positional play; playing the flop in all positions with a pair, two pair, trips, overcards, draws, made and nothing hands; turn and river play; how to read the board; avoiding trash hands; using the check-raise; bluffing, stereotypes, much more. Includes quizzes with answers. Terrific book. 176 pages, 5 1/2 x 8 1/2, paperback, $24.95.

**WINNING POKER FOR THE SERIOUS PLAYER** by Edwin Silberstang - New edition! More than 100 actual examples provide tons of advice on beating 7 Card Stud, Texas Hold 'Em, Draw Poker, Loball, High-Low and more than 10 other variations. Silberstang analyzes the essentials of being a great player; reading tells, analyzing tables, playing position, mastering the art of deception, creating fear at the table. Also, psychological tactics, when to play aggressive or slow play, or fold, expert plays, more. Colorful glossary included. 288 pages, 6 x 9, perfect bound, $16.95.

**WINNER'S GUIDE TO TEXAS HOLD 'EM POKER** by Ken Warren - This comprehensive book on beating hold 'em shows serious players how to play every hand from every position with every type of flop. Learn the 14 categories of starting hands, the 10 most common hold 'em tells, how to evaluate a game for profit, and more! Over 50,000 copies in print. 256 pages, 5 1/2 x 8 1/2, paperback, $14.95.

**KEN WARREN TEACHES TEXAS HOLD 'EM** by Ken Warren - In 33 comprehensive yet easy-to-read chapters, you'll learn absolutely everything about the great game of Texas hold 'em poker. You'll learn to play from every position, at every stage of a hand. You'll master a simple but thorough system for keeping records and understanding odds. And you'll gain expert advice on raising, stealing blinds, avoiding tells, playing for jackpots, bluffing, tournament play, and much more. 416 pages, 6 x 9, $24.95.

**Order Toll-Free 1-800-577-WINS or go to cardozapub.com**

# THE CHAMPIONSHIP BOOKS
## POWERFUL BOOKS YOU MUST HAVE

**CHAMPIONSHIP OMAHA (Omaha High-Low, Pot-limit Omaha, Limit High Omaha)** by T. J. Cloutier & Tom McEvoy. Clearly-written strategies and powerful advice from Cloutier and McEvoy who have won four World Series of Poker titles in Omaha tournaments. Powerful advice shows you how to win at low-limit and high-stakes games, how to play against loose and tight opponents, and the differing strategies for rebuy and freezeout tournaments. Learn the best starting hands, when slowplaying a big hand is dangerous, what danglers are and why winners don't play them, why pot-limit Omaha is the only poker game where you sometimes fold the nuts on the flop and are correct in doing so and overall, how can you win a lot of money at Omaha! 230 pages, photos, illustrations, $39.95.

**CHAMPIONSHIP STUD (Seven-Card Stud, Stud 8/or Better and Razz)** by Dr. Max Stern, Linda Johnson, and Tom McEvoy. The authors, who have earned millions of dollars in major tournaments and cash games, eight World Series of Poker bracelets and hundreds of other titles in competition against the best players in the world show you the winning strategies for medium-limit side games as well as poker tournaments and a general tournament strategy that is applicable to any form of poker. Includes give-and-take conversations between the authors to give you more than one point of view on how to play poker. 200 pages, hand pictorials, photos. $29.95.

**CHAMPIONSHIP HOLD'EM** by T. J. Cloutier & Tom McEvoy. Hard-hitting hold'em the way it's played today in both limit cash games and tournaments. Get killer advice on how to win more money in rammin'-jammin' games, kill-pot, jackpot, shorthanded, and other types of cash games. You'll learn the thinking process before the flop, on the flop, on the turn, and at the river with specific suggestions for what to do when good or bad things happen plus 20 illustrated hands with play-by-play analyses. Specific advice for rocks in tight games, weaklings in loose games, experts in solid games, how hand values change in jackpot games, when you should fold, check, raise, reraise, check-raise, slowplay, bluff, and tournament strategies for small buy-in, big buy-in, rebuy, incremental add-on, satellite and big-field major tournaments. Wow! Easy-to-read and conversational, if you want to become a lifelong winner at limit hold'em, you need this book! 320 Pages, Illustrated, Photos. $39.95

**CHAMPIONSHIP NO-LIMIT & POT LIMIT HOLD'EM** by T. J. Cloutier & Tom McEvoy The definitive guide to winning at two of the world's most exciting poker games! Written by eight time World Champion players T. J. Cloutier (1998 Player of the Year) and Tom McEvoy (the foremost author on tournament strategy) who have won millions of dollars playing no-limit and pot-limit hold'em in cash games and major tournaments around the world. You'll get all the answers here - no holds barred - to your most important questions: How do you get inside your opponents' heads and learn how to beat them at their own game? How can you tell how much to bet, raise, and reraise in no-limit hold'em? When can you bluff? How do you set up your opponents in pot-limit hold'em so that you can win a monster pot? What are the best strategies for winning no-limit and pot-limit tournaments, satellites, and supersatellites? You get rock-solid and inspired advice from two of the most recognizable figures in poker — advice that you can bank on. If you want to become a winning player, a champion, you must have this book. 209 pages, paperback, illustrations, photos. $39.95

**Order Toll-Free 1-800-577-WINS or use order form on page 239**

# GRI'S PROFESSIONAL VIDEO POKER STRATEGY
## Win Money at Video Poker! With the Odds!

**At last,** for the **first time,** and for **serious players** only, the GRI **Professional Video Poker** strategy is released so you too can play to win! **You read it right** - this strategy gives you the **mathematical advantage** over the casino and what's more, it's **easy to learn!**

**PROFESSIONAL STRATEGY SHOWS YOU HOW TO WIN WITH THE ODDS** - This **powerhouse strategy,** played for **big profits** by an **exclusive** circle of **professionals,** people who make their living at the machines, is now made available to you! You too can win - with the odds - and this **winning strategy** shows you how!

**HOW TO PLAY FOR A PROFIT** - You'll learn the **key factors** to play on a **pro level**: which machines will turn you a profit, break-even and win rates, hands per hour and average win per hour charts, time value, team play and more! You'll also learn big play strategy, alternate jackpot play, high and low jackpot play and key strategies to follow.

**WINNING STRATEGIES FOR ALL MACHINES** - This **comprehensive, advanced pro package** not only shows you how to win money at the 8-5 progressives, but also, the **winning strategies** for 10s or better, deuces wild, joker's wild, flat-top, progressive and special options features.

**BE A WINNER IN JUST ONE DAY** - In just one day, after learning our strategy, you will have the skills to **consistently win money** at video poker - with the odds. The strategies are easy to use under practical casino conditions.

**FREE BONUS - PROFESSIONAL PROFIT EXPECTANCY FORMULA ($15 VALUE)** - For serious players, we're including this free bonus essay which explains the professional profit expectancy principles of video poker and how to relate them to real dollars and cents in your game.

To order send just $50 by check or money order to:
Cardoza Publishing, P.O. Box 1500, Cooper Station, New York, NY 10276

# VIDEOS BY MIKE CARO
## THE MAD GENIUS OF POKER

### CARO'S PRO POKER TELLS

The long-awaited two-video set is a powerful scientific course on how to use your opponents' gestures, words and body language to read their hands and win all their money. These carefully guarded poker secrets, filmed with 63 poker notables, will revolutionize your game. It reveals when opponents are bluffing, when they aren't, and why. Knowing what your opponent's gestures mean, and protecting them from knowing yours, gives you a huge winning edge. An absolute must buy! $59.95.

### CARO'S MAJOR POKER SEMINAR

The legendary "Mad Genius" is at it again, giving poker advice in VHS format. This new tape is based on the inaugural class at Mike Caro University of Poker, Gaming and Life strategy. The material given on this tape is based on many fundamentals introduced in Caro's books, papers, and articles and is prepared in such a way that reinforces concepts old and new. Caro's style is easy-going but intense with key concepts stressed and repeated. This tape will improve your play. 60 Minutes. $24.95.

### CARO'S POWER POKER SEMINAR

This powerful video shows you how to win big money using the little-known concepts of world champion players. This advice will be worth thousands of dollars to you every year, even more if you're a big money player! After 15 years of refusing to allow his seminars to be filmed, Caro presents entertaining but serious coverage of his long-guarded secrets. Contains the most profitable poker advice ever put on video. 62 Minutes! $39.95.

**Order Toll-Free 1-800-577-WINS or use order form on page 239**

## CARDOZA PUBLISHING ONLINE

**For the latest in poker, gambling, chess, backgammon, and games
by the world's top authorities and writers**

## www.cardozapub.com

To find out about our latest publications and products, to order books and software from third parties, or simply to keep aware of our latest activities in the world or poker, gambling, and other games of chance and skill:

1. Go online: www.cardozapub.com
2. Use E-Mail: cardozapub@aol.com
3. Call toll free: 800-577-WINS (800-577-9467)

# BOOKS BY MIKE CARO
## THE MAD GENIUS OF POKER

**CARO'S BOOK OF POKER TELLS (THE BODY LANGUAGE OF POKER)** - Finally! Mike Caro's classic book is now revised and back in print! This long-awaited revision by the Mad Genius of Poker takes a detailed look at the art and science of tells, the physical mannerisms which giveaway a  player's hand. Featuring photo illustrations of poker players in action along with Caro's explanations about when players are bluffing and when they're not, these powerful eye-opening ideas can give you the decisive edge at the table! This invaluable book should be in every player's library! 320 pages! $24.95.

**CARO'S GUIDE TO DOYLE BRUNSON'S SUPER SYSTEM** - Working with World Champion Doyle Brunson, the legendary Mike Caro has created a fresh look to the "Bible" of all poker books, adding new and personal insights that help you understand the original work. Caro breaks 36 concepts into either "Analysis, Commentary, Concept, Mission, Play-By-Play, Psychology, Statistics, Story, or Strategy. Lots of illustrations and winning concepts give even more value to this great work. 86 pages, 8 1/2 x 11, stapled. $19.95.

**CARO'S FUNDAMENTAL SECRETS OF WINNING POKER** - The world's foremost poker theoretician and strategist presents the essential strategies, concepts, and secret winning plays that comprise the very foundation of winning poker play. Shows how to win more from weak players, equalize stronger players, bluff a bluffer, win big pots, where to sit against weak players,  the six factors of strategic table image. Includes selected tips on hold 'em, 7 stud, draw, lowball, tournaments, more. 160 Pages, 5 1/2 x 8 1/2, perfect bound, $12.95.

Call Toll Free (800)577-WINS or Use Coupon Below to Order Books, Videos & Software